HISTORY OF THE
AMERICAN WEST

HISTORY OF THE
AMERICAN WEST

Robin May

Exeter Books

NEW YORK

Dedication
To Leland Sonnichsen

Apart from acknowledging my debt to the authors whose books are listed in the bibliography, I must also thank the following who have been especially generous in helping me increase my knowledge of the Old West as well as those who have shown me it as it is today – Joseph Snell, Nyle Miller and Tim Bannon of Kansas; Fredie Steve Harris of Texas; Katharine Halverson of Wyoming; Ed Hartsook, Dick Dillon, Phil and Linken Ault, and Andrew Rolle of California; and Everett Brownsey and William Shillingberg of Arizona. Fellow members of the English Westerners Society who have given me expert advice down the years include Allan Radbourne on the Apache Wars, Jeff Burton on Jesse James, Colin Rickards on the Lincoln County War, and Joseph G. Rosa on Wild Bill Hickok and on firearms.

Photographic acknowledgements

The Anschutz Collection, Denver, Colorado 6, 9, 15, 78, 198-199 top; Arizona Historical Society Library 158 left, 239; Colorado Historical Society 83; Denver Public Library, Western History Department 49, 56, 84, 89 bottom; Huntington Library, San Marino, California 176 top; IPC, London Terry Hadler 125 bottom; Kansas State Historical Society, Topeka 52, 70, 95, 96, 108-109, 118, 126-127, 130-131, 150 centre, 166, 217; E. Dixon Larson Collection, Utah 125 top; Library of Congress, Washington D.C. 26-27, 181 bottom; Robin May, London 142, 147, 148 top, 163 bottom, 216 bottom, 247; Minnesota Historical Society 198 bottom; Missouri State Historical Society 116; Museum of New Mexico 145; National Archives, Washington D.C. 8, 10, 11, 18, 32, 55, 61 top, 71, 82, 156, 160-161, 184-185, 187, 203, 205 top, 210, 212 top, 214, 218, 225, 227, 228-229, 234 bottom, 235, 236, 237, 238, 242-243, 248, 249; Peter Newark's Western Americana, Bath 12, 16-17, 19, 20-21, 23, 24, 25, 26, 28, 29, 30, 31, 33, 34, 35, 36, 37, 38, 39 left, 40, 41, 42-43, 44, 45, 46, 47, 48-49, 50, 51, 53, 54, 57, 58-59, 60, 62-63, 64, 65, 66, 67, 69 (published with the permission of Exxon Corporation), 72, 73 bottom, 74, 75, 79, 80, 81, 85, 86, 88, 89 top, 90, 92, 93, 94, 98, 99, 101, 102, 103, 105, 107, 110-111, 112-113, 114, 115, 117, 119, 120, 121, 124, 128, 129, 132, 135, 136-137, 139, 141, 143 top, 146, 150 bottom, 152, 153, 155, 159, 162, 163 top, 164, 165, 167, 168-169, 170, 171, 172, 173, 174-175, 176 bottom, 177, 178, 180, 181 top, 182-183, 186, 188, 190, 191, 192-193, 194, 195, 196-197, 200, 201, 202, 205 bottom, 206-207, 208-209, 212 bottom, 213, 215 top, 216 top, 219, 220-221, 222, 226, 231, 232, 233, 234 top, 244, 245, 246, 250; Oklahoma Historical Society 158 right; Public Archives of Canada 87, 91; Smithsonian Institution, National Anthropological Archives, Washington D.C. 22, 39 right, 215 bottom, 224, 230, 252; Texas State Archives 133; Utah State Historical Society 61 bottom; Wells Fargo Bank, History Room, San Francisco 73 top, 76, 77, 140; Western History Collections, University of Oklahoma 68, 97, 100, 104, 123, 240; Western History Research Center, University of Wyoming 148 bottom, 150 top; Wyoming State Archives, Museums and Historical Department 106, 149 bottom, 204; Oliver Yates Collection 142, 223.

Front cover
Attack at Dawn, Charles Schreyvogel (The Thomas Gilcrease Institute of American History and Art, Tulsa, Oklahoma)
Back cover
Photograph of the Hayden Survey of the Western Territories, 1870-1872 (National Archives, Washington D.C.)
Title spread
Across the Continent: westward the course of Empire takes its way, Currier and Ives print (Peter Newark's Western Americana, Bath)
Endpapers
The Hold Up, Frederic Remington (Peter Newark's Western Americana, Bath)

First published in USA 1984
by Exeter Books
Distributed by Bookthrift
Exeter is a trademark of Simon & Schuster, Inc.
Bookthrift is a registered trademark of Simon & Schuster, Inc.
New York, New York

Prepared by
Deans International Publishing
52-54 Southwark Street, London SE1 1UA
A division of The Hamlyn Publishing Group Limited
London · New York · Sydney · Toronto

CONTENTS

INTRODUCTION

Despite the efforts of films and books to prove otherwise, there was little that was romantic about the Old West except for the scenery. Yet the events of those decades was something far grander than romance. The story of the West is an epic one and it remains *the* American epic, not just in the United States, but for millions around the world.

The majority of books about the West concentrate on the trans-Mississippi West, especially the period after the end of the Civil War in 1865 to the turn of the century, the period of the 'Wild West'. This is reasonable enough except for two facts – that there had already been even wilder Wests, and that the stormy years following the Civil War were the culmination of a process that had started over 300 years earlier in the Southwest and almost as long ago in the East. So it will be in those periods that this book will start, following a chapter about the coming of the first peoples to the Americas long before the white men, and how these Native Americans developed life styles and attitudes that would lead to tragic conflicts with white men.

Robin May
Wimbledon, England

George Catlin's painting of a Mandan Mystery Lodge. The Mandans, who lived along the Missouri, were almost wiped out by smallpox in 1837.

CHAPTER ONE
THE FIRST AMERICANS

Some 30,000 years before Europeans 'discovered' the New World, the ancestors of today's Native Americans truly found it. Before that moment, the Americas were empty of human life. Only the remains of *Homo sapiens* have been found there.

Columbus, thinking he had reached the Indies – India – in 1492, understandably misnamed the peoples he met, but the name 'Indians' will be used throughout this book because it is correct historically even though 'Native American' is now quite widely used.

It is generally agreed that the new arrivals to the continent came from Asia by way of the Bering Strait, a distance of less than 60 miles. How they came is not known, but during the last ice age the strait was frozen over, an event that can occur even during a severe winter. Neither do we know why they came, simple human curiosity being perhaps the most appropriate answer until we know otherwise.

The southward march to the tip of South America must have continued for thousands of years, with the immigrants finding temporary or permanent homes along the way. While Central and South America are not the concern of this book, it must be noted that the Maya, Aztec, Inca and other cultures of those regions grew to be more advanced than those in what are now the United States and Canada. North America remained thinly populated, with perhaps a million inhabitants altogether, while Mexico alone may have had as many as 15 million at the height of the Aztec culture around the 15th century.

At the fringes of Mexican civilization were the pueblos (towns) of

Right: The Indian Village of Acoma *by Jules Tavernier.*

Left: A Kaivavit Paiute father and his daughter in front of their home, photographed by Clement Powell in 1872.

today's Southwest, busy villages several storeys high, built on mesas, in cliff caverns and on flat ground. The 11–13th centuries were the high noon of these examples of communal living. When the Spaniards arrived in the 16th century, the communities had begun to decline, perhaps from drought, perhaps because of warlike peoples from the North, ancestors of the Apache and Navaho. We may never know the reasons. Yet some survive to this day. As we shall see in the next chapter, it was the Southwest which was to be the first region of the American West to experience European invaders.

White attitudes to Indians tended to depend on geography: on the Frontier, where they were called 'painted fiends' or 'savages', further east, variants on two linked themes, 'the noble savage' and 'the downtrodden native'. Before land-seeking settlers arrived and inevitably poisoned relations between the races, contacts, as white explorers and travellers found, could be friendly enough. George Catlin, the artist, roamed the West painting some of the 'wildest' tribes on the continent in the 1830s and came to no harm. A generation later his journeys could have been suicidal.

Since the 1950s, conscience has made many Americans reconsider the plight of the Indians. Yet popular knowledge of the Old West has not increased. The Indian has been portrayed in some places as an ideal ecologist, a master of communal living, in touch with the natural world, a warrior who preferred peace, and only reluctantly went to war. As regards their interpersonal relationships however, the elderly were often harshly treated, and in most tribes women

were very much second class citizens, working long hours in the fields and in the home while the men hunted, fought or talked. Yet what the Indian did have was finely summed up by Frederick William Turner III in his *The Portable North American Reader*: 'The Indian never lost sight of the fact that all this [the harshness of Indian life] was distinctively, essentially, radically human, that he was human and thus part of the universal community of the living.'

The various tribes, widespread though they were, shared so much in common that the differences between them are more properly stressed first. Property and status are often regarded as solely white concerns, but the coastal Indians of the Northwest respected them, too. As for the Natchez, their class structure was more rigid than that of Victorian England's, with a Sun God at the summit while at the bottom of the social pyramid was a class known as 'Stinkards'. Again, it is common knowledge that the coming of the horse turned the Plains Indians into nomads, but although the Caddo and the Mandan were horseriding buffalo hunters in the 19th century, they still farmed and lived in settlements. As for appearance, the Plains Indian is regarded as typical, but there were many different Indian 'looks' and variations of skin colour, and there still are. As regards languages, the sign language of the Plains was absolutely vital. Indians have six main language groups and there were hundreds of different languages across the continent, some of which have now died out.

Yet Indians everywhere shared certain beliefs that helped make clashes with the white man, especially Anglo-

Left: An unidentified Indian from a Southeast Idaho reservation, 1897.

Right: Timothy O'Sullivan's Navaho Group, *photographed in the Canyon de Chailly in Arizona in 1873.*

American man, inevitable. These clashes were fundamental and had nothing to do with the tools and weapons that the whites introduced – which were eagerly taken up by the Indians. The difference lay in opposing attitudes to the land.

To the Indians, the Earth was their mother, not something that was owned, bought or sold. It was a divine gift given to humans and animals, to be farmed, hunted over and fought over, but not to be possessed as the whites possessed it, in small 'plots'. It was a corollary of this natural philosophy that all living things – all animals – were the Indians' brothers and sisters. That they hunted animals to live did not alter this relationship.

They were religious peoples, and 'medicine' protected them in peace and in war. Their actual medicine was in many cases in advance of that of the whites until a century ago, in some cases later than that. Some 200 drugs used by Indians have been accepted as valuable by white authorities. In 1780 the Mohawk Joseph Brant was watched by one of his white captives curing himself of 'the fever and ague' by drinking rattlesnake soup, while his sister Molly cured the Lieutenant-Governor of Upper Canada (Ontario), Colonel John Simcoe, as Mrs. Simcoe related in her diary. He had had an appalling cough, splitting headaches and a total loss of appetite for over a month. Then 'Capt. Brant's sister prescribed a Root – I believe it is calamus – which really relieved his Cough in a very short time'.

The democratic communal life of the Indian had one drawback. Democracy all too often led to anarchy in time of war. Indian war chiefs hardly ever had the power of white generals, rarely having the overall control of junior officers. So important was personal freedom to the Indian that warriors too often wrecked an attack to make their mark. When war was the greatest of all games, with tribe attacking tribe, this did not matter so much, but against white troops under strict discipline and with better weapons it could be disastrous. Great leaders who tried to go further and united many tribes, as Pontiac and Tecumseh did for a time, suffered even more from this emphasis on personal freedom.

Naturally, the coming of the horse made the conduct of war faster and even more exciting. All the Plains Indians were horsemen by the late 18th century, joyously riding the descendants of escaped or captured Spanish horses. Instead of being ponderous hand-to-hand matches, fighting was transformed into a mounted contest not unlike the tournaments of medieval times. To touch an enemy with a coup stick, then retire safely, was an even greater achievement than to kill him. This was no way to fight the US Army on the open Plains, splendid as it was. Fortunately for the Apache as we shall see, war was never a great game for them.

Torture was common, especially in the East, just as it was in Europe. The worse tribes were treated, the more brutal some of them became. All Indians admired bravery and much admired those who could endure torture. A prisoner of the Iroquois who could shout back at his tormentors was sometimes eaten to gain his strength.

What really shocked Indians was the white habit of imprisoning people. On a visit to England, Joseph Brant was so astounded to discover that

Left: Comanche Catching Wild Horses *by Catlin.*

even debtors were incarcerated that he said he would rather endure the worst tortures at the stake than be imprisoned. Some Indians killed themselves rather than endure captivity, others killed themselves in prison.

Even the most warlike tribes enjoyed periods of peace, and before alcohol – introduced by whites – sapped the fibre of so many unfortunate Indians, life in an Indian camp had many joys, so many in fact that captives, even ones taken when no longer children, were often reluctant to be returned to the joys of civilization. Although in many tribes the women had to work too hard, children, especially boys, normally had a spoiled, carefree existence. In some tribes, notably in the East, women had real political power. There were even some women chiefs.

With perhaps a million or less Indians in what is now the United States, it was impossible for the Indians to hold their lands. The fact that they did not, and that many do not now want to assimilate with the whites, makes their story more tragic. The Indians lost their old way of life, having forgotten an even older way when they had been farmers before the coming of the horse.

One man, who lived at a time when it seemed that the Indians were doomed to extinction, was the great Western artist, Charles Russell. He was also a cowboy and he lived with the Blackfoot for a spell. He paid the Indian a tribute that has rarely been bettered:

The Red man was the true American. They have almost all gone, but will never be forgotten. The history of how they fought for their country is written in blood, a stain that time cannot grind out. Their God was the sun, their church all out doors. Their only book was nature and they knew all the pages.

Left: Indian Encampment *by Henry F. Farny.*

CHAPTER TWO
THE COMING OF THE WHITES

To the Spaniards who had conquered Mexico and Peru nothing can have seemed impossible. Cortez, with some 500 Conquistadores plus Indian allies had toppled the mighty Aztec Empire. Pizarro, with less than 200, had conquered the Incas and seized unimaginable quantities of gold. So when news reached Mexico City that there were seven cities of gold to the north – the Seven Cities of Cibola – it caused intense excitement but surely little surprise.

Rumours had been rife from 1536 when some soldiers had come across a white man who wept with joy to see them. He was called de Vaca, and though he had Indians and a Negro with him, he had not seen a white man for eight years. In Mexico City he explained that he had survived an expedition that had attempted to conquer Florida and had had many adventures cross westwards before entering into Mexico from the north. Treasure came into his story, which electrified men who wanted to believe that another Peru lay to the north.

The Viceroy sent a Franciscan, Marcos de Niza, to check the story, and with him went de Vaca's Negro companion Estevan. The friar returned with sensational news. He had seen the golden city. Gold fever swept the city, and was not lessened when de Niza admitted he had only seen Cibola from afar. Estevan, he related, had been there, however, and found that Cibola was seven cities, not one, and governed by a single ruler. Doorways were richly paved with turquoise in this golden city, which was bigger than Mexico City. And Estevan? Dead, alas, having thrown his weight around in Cibola – which the friar had sensibly claimed for Spain from a

distance before he fled back home.

An expedition led by Francisco de Coronado started north in March 1540, consisting possibly of several thousand cavalry and infantry, plus Mexican Indian helpers and sheepherders. Father de Niza accompanied them. After a difficult march, they reached and stormed Cibola. Their firearms and horses, both unknown to the Cibolans, assured them of victory.

But where was the fabulous gold? From a distance, Cibola, the sun beating down on it, did seem built of shining palaces, but not close to. It was a town of 200 or so stone and mud houses, four storeys high, and the inhabitants were farmers. There were other small towns in the area, none of them golden.

De Niza was sent back to Mexico in disgrace, lucky to escape execution. Coronado and his Conquistadores, having started 350 years of warfare between Indians and whites in the West, pressed on past other multi-

Below: The Coronado Expedition, *painted by Frederic Remington.*

storeyed villages, still hoping for gold. Excitement mounted when an Indian told them of a place where little golden bells hung on trees – for which lie he was later strangled – and the expedition returned in failure in 1542.

Yet Coronado had triumphed as an explorer. He had gone as far north as Kansas, and as far east as Texas and Oklahoma. The Spaniards had seen and hunted buffalo; some of them became the first whites to gaze in awe at the Grand Canyon, but only a third of them survived to tell their tales. Yet they left a priceless treasure for the Indians, for some of their horses were left behind and from them, and later others, grew the herds of wild horses of the Plains. One unknown day an Indian mounted a horse and the history of warfare in the West was dramatically changed.

Meanwhile, in Florida another Spanish expedition set out westwards, led by Hernando de Soto, who had been Pizarro's second-in-command in Peru. Starting in 1539, he and his men almost reached Oklahoma, but found no riches. Yet between them, de Soto and Coronado had virtually traversed what would become the United States.

De Soto died on the banks of the Mississippi in 1542. In the West, 'New Spain', which would later cover the American Southwest and California, was extended very slowly, partly because Spanish power waned in Europe in the 17th century. Difficulties of climate and transport, and too few Spaniards on the ground, meant that Spanish claims were not matched by actual ownership. The finest colonists were Jesuit missionaries, who established a line of mission stations northwards along the coast. Further east, as we shall see, Spanish claims were to affect the advance westwards of the United States.

The French

The second European power on the North American scene was France. Jacques Cartier had sailed up the St. Lawrence river to where Quebec now stands as early as 1535, but it was Samuel Champlain who founded it as France's first colony in North America in 1608. The early French inhabitants were fur traders and fishermen rather than colonists. La Salle, who discovered the Ohio in 1669 and sailed

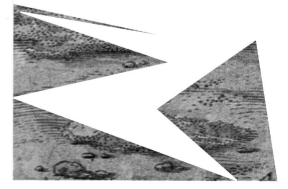

down the Mississippi in 1682, claimed the whole Mississippi Basin for France. Despite their lack of numbers, French power – though influence may be a better word – spread from the St. Lawrence to the Gulf of Mexico. For the French – explorers and traders, missionaries and soldiers – rarely sought to rob the Indians of their land, unlike the English, who were land-hungry farmers. The French government helped 'New France' by founding the Company of the West in 1664, granting it a trade monopoly and donating cash and troops. France's position appeared very strong.

The French had made one grave error, however, the culprit being Champlain himself. He had made an enemy of the great Iroquois Confederacy.

The Five Nations of the Confederacy were the Mohawk, Oneida, Onondaga, Cayuga and Seneca, who occupied a key position in what is now New York State whereby they could dominate the fur trade. They became the Six Nations in the 18th century when they allowed the Tuscarora to join them after the tribe had been driven out of the Carolinas by whites.

Champlain and two other French-

Below: Florida Indians Washing for Gold *by Theodor de Bry, 1591.*

men were out with a war party of Huron when they came upon that tribe's enemies, in this case a band of Mohawk. The Frenchmen won the skirmish by using firearms. Three Iroquois chiefs were killed, and from that moment the Five Nations became enemies of France (usually) and, later, friends of the English (as a rule). The French compounded their folly by sending some Iroquois to be slaves in Mediterranean galleys.

By the early 18th century, however, France's position in America seemed very strong. The founding of New Orleans in 1718 meant that she had a string of settlements along North America's greatest rivers, complete

with key ports. She was thinking in terms of the West at a time when her rival, England, had colonies that were united in looking towards the Atlantic and not, as yet, across the Appalachians.

The English

English vessels had reached New-foundland as early as 1497 under John Cabot, but it was clearly not to be compared with the 'Indies' that the

Below: 17th century New England settlers fighting off Indians.

Spaniards had found, complete with its gold. However, the growth of English sea power in Elizabethan times, and the lure of potential riches in both North America and the Indies, made settlement in the New World an attractive proposition. The great Sir Walter Raleigh as well as others had been attempting colony foundation since the 1580s, but it was not until 1607 that England's first successful colony was established at Jamestown, Virginia.

It had a very tough start. Many of the original 105 who landed died from disease and lack of food, and certain failure was halted mainly by the determined character of one of the colony's leaders, Captain John Smith. The colony was saved in 1610 with the arrival of its first governor, Lord De La Warr, complete with food supplies.

Another salvation was the help given to the Englishmen by Pocahontas, daughter of the local Indian chief, Powhatan. This delightful girl not only saved Smith's life when Powhatan was about to have him killed, but she also promoted racial harmony by marrying one of the Jamestown settlers, John Rolfe. (It has to be admitted that there are those who believe that Smith made up his stay-of-execution story!)

Pocahontas and her husband paid a visit to England in 1616, where she became the first Indian to cause a sensation at the Court, in London and elsewhere. Sadly, she died in 1617 just as she was due to sail for home, but many distinguished Virginians are descended from her son.

The colony's key crop was tobacco, which, because it used up land quickly, caused strained relations between the races. In 1622, the Powhatans rose against their old friends – but too late because now there were many more whites and fewer Indians, disease having cut into their numbers.

Meanwhile, in 1620, a very different band of emigrants, the Pilgrim Fathers, had landed on Cape Cod in what was to become Massachusetts. Thanksgiving Day annually celebrates their good relations with the local Indians – at first. Then, as in Virginia, war broke out – 'King Philip's War' – in 1675. Philip was to be killed, his wife and child sent to the West Indies as slaves.

Though this is not a history of the eastern seaboard, it should be noted that the Indians spared Roger Williams of Rhode Island who had dared champion Indian land rights and religious tolerance and was banished for his 'crimes'. William Penn was another famous exception, though many humbler folk, less as the years went by, had Indian friends.

The Indians could never have driven the whites back into the Atlantic except in the earliest days, and even then the latter would have returned. The world-wide conflicts between Britain and France in the 18th century never really ended with the official peace treaties in North America until 1763. That year saw the end of the Seven Years War, a struggle that had begun more than seven years earlier in America, where it is still known as the French and Indian War. At the Treaty of Paris, France abandoned her claim to Canada and all lands east of the Mississippi. Freed of the French menace, and with successive British governments making blunder after blunder, the colonists' march towards revolution began. But before the movement got into its stride, a ferocious Indian outbreak proved how slender the English hold on the continent was, except along the coastline.

Ætatis suæ 21. Aº. 1616.

Matoaks als Rebecka daughter to the mighty Prince Powhatan Emperour of Attanoughkomouck als Virginia converted and baptized in the Christian faith, and Wife to the Worⁿ Mʳ Tho: Rolff.

Left: Pochahontas in English court dress. She was given the name 'Rebecka' when she was baptized in 1614. Her famous visit to England was two years later.

Right: Cunne Shote, a great Warrior of the Cherokee Nation, *painted in London in 1762 by Francis Parsons.*

22

CHAPTER THREE
FRONTIER IN FLAMES

The famous victory of Wolfe over Montcalm on the Heights of Abraham in 1759, which cost both generals their lives, made it certain that France would lose Canada. However, not until September 1760 did General Amherst round off the conquest of 'New France'.

Amherst had proved able enough in the war, but he, more than anyone else, was responsible for the bloody explosion known as Pontiac's War. The great historian Francis Parkman called his account of the uprising *The Conspiracy of Pontiac*, but in *Pontiac and the Indian Uprising* Howard Peckham shows that the Ottawa chief did not mastermind the affair.

The French, as has been noted, were on much better terms than the English with the Indians, the Iroquois apart. British officers, Wolfe included, had little time for Indians as allies, the one exception being Sir William Johnson. This genial Irishman, who had come as a trader to the Mohawk Valley in New York province in 1738, became the greatest landowner in the American Colonies. More remarkably, despite his capacity for acquiring land, Indian land included, he got on famously with most Indians, notably the Iroquois and, especially, the Mohawk.

Johnson had become a baronet in the grim year of Braddock's defeat, by French and Indians in 1755, a defeat when Redcoats were ambushed and panicked, and where young George Washington helped save a disaster from turning into a total catastrophe. At Lake George, in New York province two months later, Johnson, leading some 3,000 Colonials and 300 Indians, most of them Mohawk, just managed to defeat a French and Indian force under a German commander

with a European reputation, Baron Dieskau, then in the French service.

Johnson, for all his knowledge of the Indians and the Frontier, and despite later successes, was regarded as a mere amateur by Amherst, and it was the latter, not an expert, who dictated Indian policy after the war. He cut off supplies of ammunition, arms, food and gifts to the Indians, and when Pontiac's war broke out in 1763, suggested that the Indian 'problem' might be solved by using infected blankets to spread smallpox among the tribes. Fortunately, this was not done. Meanwhile, the French on the Frontier encouraged the tribes to rebel, a rebellion which, though led by Pontiac, was stimulated by the Delaware Prophet. He was one of a number of visionaries who would inspire Indians right down to Wounded Knee in 1890, almost always with fatal results, however good the cause.

The rebellion started off sensationally. Every fort west of Niagara was overwhelmed except Forts Pitt and Detroit. Fort Michilimackinac was captured by cunning, Chippewa taking on Sauk at a game of lacrosse

outside the fort, watched by many of the garrison. Suddenly, a ball was hooked over the stockade. The Indians ran in after it, dropped their sticks and collected weapons that their squaws had been concealing. They then proceeded to kill traders and soldiers alike.

Settlers, some of whom would hold out later against the fury on the Frontier during the Revolution, fled in terror, refusing to help the few troops on the Frontier. Pontiac's aim of bringing back the French and driving the colonists back across the Alleghenies to the coastal regions seemed within his grasp, but Detroit held and Pontiac wasted his strength by trying to run a European style siege of the key outpost. Gradually he lost control over his loose union of tribes. Fortunately, the Southern tribes were not involved, but the danger was grim enough. Even the Iroquois split, the Seneca, the largest nation, siding with Pontiac. It needed all Johnson's skill (underrated by the British) to get Pontiac to surrender in July 1766. The chief was murdered three years later by a Peoria Indian in Illinois.

Above: Chief Pontiac and his men leaving Fort Detroit, *from the Remington painting.*

Opposite page: The Death of General Brassock in the forests of Pennsylvania in 1755.

Despite mistakes and disasters, the British under Major Gladwin had held on to Fort Detroit with the utmost tenacity, while Fort Pitt had been saved in a ferocious action at Bushy Run where the British were led by a brilliant Swiss mercenary, Colonel Henry Bouquet. In his *History of the British Army,* Sir John Fortescue wrote: 'Long though the combat has been forgotten in England, the history of the Army can show few finer performances on its own scale than this victory of a handful of English, Highlanders, and Germans, under the leadership of a Swiss Colonel.'

With the French threat now finally ended, it is as clear today as it was to a few at the time that the countdown to rebellion against the Mother Country had begun. When that rebellion did

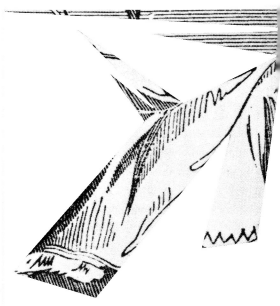

break out in 1775 a change had come over those Frontier people who had quickly fled in Pontiac's time. Not only had some 30,000 made the crossing of the Appalachian barrier, but they were prepared to stay. Many were to perish in the bitter years to come, but now there would be no general exodus when crisis, in the form of Indian warfare, wreaked havoc on them, warfare in which Britons and Loyalists would join. The Frontier war would be a nightmare for both sides, but war it would be, not a mass, panic-stricken evacuation.

The British government had drawn up a Proclamation Line in 1763 roughly along the Appalachians to confine the colonists to the eastern seaboard. It infuriated both Virginian land companies and would-be western pioneers. The line was slightly altered in 1768 – for the worst from the Indian point of view – at the Treaty of Fort Stanwix. To keep white settlers from their own land, the lordly Iroquois gave away land to the south of the Ohio as far west as the Tennessee, land they had 'owned' as overlords, allowing other tribes to hunt there. The result was a flood of white settlers and a grim future for the Shawnee and Delaware who had used those areas. There had been white men there also, 'long hunters' like Daniel Boone, Michael Stoner and Samuel Kenton, men who, unlike the average settler, learnt to fight Indians like Indians. Average or exceptional, none were concerned with proclamations or the claims of land companies, though those companies would later force

many to move on – westwards. Many would die, some would flee east again, but some survived. Their grandchildren would reach the Pacific.

This is to anticipate the result of the Revolution, which could well have been won by either side. The Frontier was to play a key role in the outcome. Racial hatred reached appalling heights in the decade before the Revolution, except in New York, where Sir William Johnson's influence held sway until his untimely death in 1774.

The Frontiersman's point of view must be understood. Any man coming back to his cabin and finding his family butchered was likely to become an Indian-hater for life. This was the period when 'The only good Indian is a dead Indian' and 'Nits make lice' – to justify killing children – were first heard. Yet white atrocities were equally appalling, and one particularly revolting feature of white tactics was to kill Indian ambassadors, a crime which was never punished on the Frontier – though this was often denied in the East. Another was to assault the nearest Indians for the crimes of others. The Mingo sub-chief Logan, who had many white friends, suffered the loss of 13 of his family, including his mother, brother and several sisters. He killed 13 whites in revenge. His followers were not so restrained. Logan's speech, a famous lament, named the wrong villain, but is a classic of its kind. Here is part of one translation of it:

I appeal to any white man to say if he ever entered Logan's cabin hungry, and he gave him not meat; if he ever came cold and naked and he clothed him not. During the course of the last long and bloody war, Logan remained idle in his cabin, an advocate for peace. Such was my love for the whites, that my countrymen pointed, as they passed, and said, 'Logan is the friend of the white man.' Colonel Cresap, the last Spring, in cold blood and unprovoked, murdered all the relations of Logan, not even sparing my women and children. There runs not a drop of my

blood in the veins of any living creature. This called on me for revenge. I have sought it; I have killed many; I have fully glutted my vengeance. For my country, I rejoice at the beams of peace; but do not harbour a thought that mine is the joy of fear. Logan never felt fear. He will not turn on his heel to save his life. Who is there to mourn for Logan? Not one.

The Revolutionary Frontier

The claim in the Declaration of Independence that George III had 'endeavoured to bring on the inhabitants of our frontiers, the merciless Indian Savages, whose known rules of warfare, is an undistinguished destruction of all ages, sexes and conditions' seems reasonable enough, but was rank hypocrisy. The first Indians to join the combatants were Stockbridge, who sided with the Rebels; the mighty Iroquois confederacy split, the Oneida siding with the Americans, mainly because of the influence of their Congregational pastor, Samuel Kirkland; Congress in secret session on May 25th, 1776 resolved to call for a direct military alliance with the Indians and authorized Washington to raise Indian allies.

Easier said than done. The English, apart from the fact that they seemed the likely winners – agents did good work to spread that gospel – could point out that Indian land was safer under them than greedy American settlers. The Indians had come to rely on English traders for goods and weapons, and were far more likely to trust agents of the Crown than those of the Congress.

Before concentrating on the northern frontier where Indians were in a position to affect the course of the war, it must be stressed that the Southern Frontier was in turmoil throughout the war, the tribes being enraged by the surge eastwards of a new, fiercer, more determined breed of Frontier people.

The newcomers proved too much for the Cherokee who in 1777 were forced to give up much of their land. It was a hard life being an agent of the King on the Southern frontier, especially when Spain declared war on Britain in 1779 and yet more had to be spent on the Creek, Chickasaw, and the vanquished Cherokee. There were many Loyalists in the South, so a bitter civil war raged, made worse by traditional feuds.

Apart from an abortive attack on Charleston in 1776, there had been no 'official' war in the South, but from 1778 it was wracked with particularly savage warfare because tough and angry Loyalist regiments had come South with the British regulars. The Carolinas suffered bloody civil war because of them, and in the western reaches of the Southern ex-colonies the nightmare was even worse. It was a nightmare that went on well after the British defeat at Yorktown, wrongly thought to be the virtual end of the Revolution. The people of the Caroli-

Below: Fort Boonesborough as it must have looked in 1778 when it was besieged by Shawnee. It was reconstructed in the 1970s.

nas, Tory or Whig, Loyalist or Patriot, suffered in the same way as their counterparts suffered in the most fought over area of all, the Mohawk Valley.

Blood and Fire in the Valley

Nowhere was the race for Indian support more frantic than on the New York frontier. The racial mixture along the Mohawk itself was remarkable with Dutch landowners where the river flows into the Hudson, the grandchildren of German immigrants in considerable numbers along the river, Scotch-Irish settlers, even a large body of Highlanders from Scotland who were both tenants of and bodyguards to Sir John Johnson, Sir William's son and successor. There were also the Mohawk, less than a hundred of them now warriors, but colossal in prestige, and the Oneidas. The rest of the Six Nations were outside the main settlement zone.

The importance of this area was immense, not just strategically – there was only one short portage between the Hudson and Lake Ontario – but economically. The fertile Mohawk Valley was to be the breadbasket of Washington's Army. The devastation of the valley by Loyalists and Indians later in the war was not merely revenge for their being driven from their homes but first-rate tactics. The raids seemed likely to starve Washington's men into submission. Fortunately, for the Patriots, the Six Nations, as noted, were to split, the Mohawk, Seneca and Cayuga supporting the King, the Oneidas, siding with the Americans, along with many Tuscarora. Most of the Onondaga remained neutral. The Confederacy was fatally divided, the sacred council fire, signifying unity, at Onondaga being put out.

A number of Iroquois were to render sterling service to their people and the British in the war, among them the Seneca war chief, Sayenqueraghta, but the most famous Indian leader in the North was Joseph Brant – Thayendanegea – the great Mohawk.

Born in 1742, Brant had become part of the household of Sir William

Above: Joseph Brant – Thayandanegea – the great Mohawk, painted by Romney in London in 1776. After the Revolution the Mohawks moved to what is now Ontario, where Brant died in 1807.

Johnson when he was a boy, his sister being Johnson's last mistress, ranking as a wife. Brant first saw action in the French and Indian War. He went to a white school for a time and officially became an Anglican, helping to translate St. Mark's Gospel into Mohawk. In November 1775 he sailed to England with Guy Johnson, Sir William's nephew who succeeded him as Superintendant of Indian Affairs in the North. Brant's mission was to check the advantages of an Iroquois alliance with the King. The result was a promise of protection of Indian land rights in the future in exchange for an Indian alliance with the Crown in the Revolution. He was lionized in London, and was painted by Romney and interviewed by James Boswell.

Back in America – where he distinguished himself at the Battle of Long

Island and made some very influential English friends – Brant returned to the Iroquois country, hoping to stir the Six Nations into action. British opinion, including that of officers in the Indian service, was split on the use of Indians, but from 1777 they were to play an important role in the British war effort on the northern Frontier. In the ferocious battle at Oriskany, part of the 1777 strategy which finally collapsed when Burgoyne surrendered at Saratoga, it was Brant who

organized the ambush at Oriskany into which the local Rebel militia marched. Their commander, Nicholas Herkimer, had two brothers in the Loyalist force attacking him: it was that sort of war along the Mohawk. In the event, both sides claimed a victory in a battle which, given the numbers involved, was the bloodiest of the whole war. Tactically it was a British victory because the Rebels failed to relieve nearby Fort Stanwix, but as the British general St. Leger failed to reach Burgoyne and was forced to retreat, it was a long term defeat. Both Brants had distinguished themselves, for Brant's sister Molly, seeing the Rebel army advancing, had dispatched Indian runners to warn St. Leger.

The next year the full Indian and Tory fury hit the Mohawk Valley. Seething with hatred, racially mixed bands swept across the once fertile province reducing it to ruin. The local militia was virtually helpless as Indians under Brant and other chiefs, and Loyalists leaders including the Butlers, father and son, fought to win their homeland back. Contrary to legend, it was not at first so very bloody, John Butler's notorious raid

on Wyoming, Pennsylvania, in 1778 being a straight military victory. Brant, who was later blamed for alleged atrocities, was not even there. The first real nightmare happened at Cherry Valley in November 1778, when neither Brant nor young Walter Butler could restrain bitter Seneca who had been unjustly accused of atrocities. This time there were indeed some.

In 1779, Washington ordered an attack on the Iroquois homeland using troops he could ill afford to lose. General Sullivan was given the command and did indeed destroy the homes and farms of the most westerly of the Nations, notably the Seneca's. But he failed to march on and destroy Fort Niagara, the operational base of Loyalist and Indian activity. The nightmare continued in 1780 and until many months after the British defeat at Yorktown in October 1781.

When the terms of the peace treaty reached the Frontier late in 1783 it was found that the Indians had been left out of it altogether. A Whig Government had replaced Lord North and was, as the Whigs had been all along, sympathetic to the America cause. The whole Northwest – the Old North-

Above: Redskin and Redcoat, *a poster for the 1976 exhibition at Greenwich, England, '1776 – The British Story of the American Revolution.'*

west as far as the Mississippi – had been handed over to the new Republic. Appalled British officials started playing for time until the Government – a new one – decided to stall in handing over the key 'posts' in the Northwest. There was to be plenty of action before the border question was finally settled. Meanwhile, Joseph Brant headed for London again to try and repair some of the damage done to the Indian cause.

The Kentuckian

Just as Fort Niagara was the hornets' nest from which the Anglo-Indian assault on the New York Frontier was directed, Fort Detroit was the headquarters of the battle to drive Kentuckians and others back across the mountains and to deter the Americans from making contact with friendly Spaniards along the Mississippi as well as potentially friendly Frenchmen who might be expected to prefer

Americans to Britons.

The commandant at Fort Detroit was Lieutenant Colonel Henry Hamilton, unaffectionately known as 'Hair Buyer' by Americans liable to lose theirs thanks to his activities. If he did offer money for scalps, he was, in fact, following an old British, French and American custom!

Hamilton was an able man who had the misfortune to encounter a Frontier genius in the shape of George Rogers Clark, Virginian born and now in his mid-twenties. He put his plan to hit British supply centres in the 'Illinois Country' – now Illinois, Ohio and Indiana – to leading Virginians, including Thomas Jefferson. Virginia's Burgesses were told that the money he needed was for the defence of Kentucky, not for such a bold plan as the capture of the key base of Kaskaskia south of St. Louis on the Mississippi, and, perhaps, Detroit itself.

Clark set off down the Ohio with less than 200 men on June 26th, 1778. They hid their boats below the mouth

Below: Americans storming a British redoubt at Yorktown, 1781. On the Frontier the war continued.

Above: Scalping for profit was never official British policy, but Indians brought in scalps anyway and went away with goods – which no doubt seemed a reward for scalping.

of the Tennessee River and, after a grim trek during which their food ran out, took Kaskaskia, which was unguarded, without a fight. Other posts also fell without resistance.

Knowing the risks despite his success, Clark spoke to delegations from many tribes with such skill that he gained a truce that held for a time.

Meanwhile, Hamilton, an able Frontier commander, led a mixed force on an appallingly difficult winter march to retake a key post, Vincennes, whose people quickly rallied to the King! The small American garrison wisely surrendered. Both wilderness commanders had done well.

Refusing to be worried by the disaster, Clark set off with some 180 men on another terrible march, some

Above: Charles McBarron's painting of Colonel Henry Hamilton surrendering the British stronghold of Vincennes to George Rogers Clark.

Left: George Rogers Clark leading his men towards Vincennes in 1778, where the British Commander, 'Hair-Buyer' Hamilton, was captured. Clark was one of the few leaders on either side who showed signs of military genius.

of it through shoulder deep icy water. Nearing his objective, he was told by a captured Frenchman that Hamilton had no idea that the Americans were near. So, despite a shortage of ammunition, Clark decided to attack that night, though he had been told that 200 Indians had just joined Hamilton.

The key point was Fort Sackville, two miles from the town. Clark sent a message to Hamilton who was there telling him what he was going to do — take the fort that night. Friends of the Americans should stay indoors, friends of the English should go to the fort. Then he and his men marched through Vincennes beating their drums. Some headed down side streets to give the impression of numbers.

Soon, townspeople were helping the Americans to find ammunition, and Indians, hearing of what was going on in town, quietly left the fort. Yet there were still 100 men in the fort, plus artillery, its impact lessened because Clark's men had dug themselves in during the night. In the morning, despite the shelling, they picked off the gunners until later in the day Hamilton surrendered. In a war not notable for brilliant operations on either side, this was an outstanding achievement by Clark.

This exceptionally gifted young man should have become even more well-known after the war. Sadly, his reputation in Virginia was maligned by the brilliant scoundrel, possibly traitor, James Wilkinson, who wanted the honest Clark out of the way. So his nation never made the most of his talents and his state never paid him the fortune he was owed in back pay, and for advancing his own money to supply his troops in a post-war campaign. Every American knows of his youngest brother, William Clark of Lewis and Clark fame. Few have heard of the brilliant feats of the conqueror of the Old Northwest.

33

CHAPTER FOUR
FAREWELL TO THE EAST

Left: The Seminole leader Osceola, an Indian of storybook nobility, who was treacherously captured and died in prison in 1838.

Twenty-one years after the Revolution ended the Lewis and Clark expedition, described in the next chapter, set out from St. Louis. It is the starting point of many books about the West, yet at that time the story of the first West was by no means over. The problem inherited by the United States from the British – how to remove, to the white man's satisfaction, all Indians from the East – had still to be finally solved. There was still an Indian Question.

Officially, the lands north of the Ohio were now ripe for taming and settlement, but the British showed no inclination to give up any of their posts, which included Detroit, Michilimackinac and also Niagara and Oswego in New York. A new government, as noted, had replaced the Whigs, whose representatives at the treaty talks in Paris had only drawn the line at surrendering Canada!

Thus the Northwest Question was far from settled. Joseph Brant was back from a second, even more triumphant, trip to London – though without cast-iron guarantees of support. The Foreign Secretary, Lord Sydney, however, valued the Indians as 'allies' and approved of Brant's plan to form an Indian confederation.

Brant and those Iroquois who wished to go settled on the Grand River in Ontario, a spot that reminded them a little of their old home. They had been promised land by General Haldimand, who had been Governor General of Canada when the war ended. Now the Iroquois were finally split, those who went to Canada having the best of a poor bargain.

Meanwhile, what passed as an American army – militia plus a few regulars – was first whipped by Indians led by Little Turtle of the Miami and Blue Jacket of the Shawnee in 1790, and then, in 1791, almost annihilated. The incompetent General St. Clair suffered 600 dead, a far greater disaster than the Little Bighorn in 1876. Neither battle has a name. They are cited as Harmar's defeat and St. Clair's disaster. In 1794, the unfortunate President Washington had better luck. 'Mad Anthony' Wayne, a general with a very fine record in the Revolution, crushed an Indian army under Little Turtle at a spot, once hit by a tornado, called Fallen Timbers. The survivors hoped to find succour in nearby Fort Miami, but Major William Campbell, fearing an international incident, refused the unfortunate refugees shelter. It was the end of an era.

Abandoned by the British, who were too thin on the ground to help them, even should they now want to, the Indians finally surrendered the old Northwest, while the British, too, pulled out from their posts in 1796 as settlers flooded in. Further south, 100,000 or more whites had already crossed into Kentucky and Tennessee.

Meanwhile, Joseph Brant was en-

Above: An army under General St. Clair suffered a most catastrophic defeat at the hands of Indians in 1791. The Americans lost 600 dead, a far greater number than at Custer's Last Stand. The unnamed battle is known as St. Clair's Disaster.

Destruction of Indian Villages.

Left: During and after the Revolution many Indian towns were destroyed and farms laid waste. Few Indians remained in the East – and the pressure continued.

35

gaged in a long battle with the Canadian authorities over the Indians' right to sell their land to white men – including men who had fought alongside Brant in his white and Indian strike force in New York. He never won his fight – the victory came in his son's time long after his father's great dream of an Indian buffer state had died. Yet his later dream of a smaller barrier came true after his death,

Mohawk and Loyalists combining to defeat invading Americans in the War of 1812.

Tecumseh

When the War of 1812 broke out, the Shawnee Tecumseh's career was in decline. As inspiring a figure as any in American history, he was a man of exceptional vision and stature. As land

was taken from tribe after tribe in the 1790s, the young Tecumseh was making his name as a warrior. In the early years of the new century he began to preach unity to tribes and so inspired them that the old dream again seemed a possibility. That it was too late does not detract from his achievement. He vainly told the Indians that they must hold the Ohio as an Indian border, yet such was his power that whites began

Right: The great Tecumseh's brother, known as 'the Prophet'.

Below: The Battle of Fallen Timbers in August 1794 forced the Indians to abandon the Old Northwest. Artist: Charles McBarron.

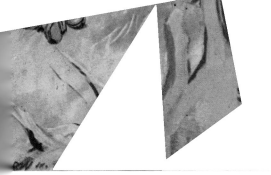

to be seriously worried. Admirable men like Thomas Jefferson might preach the rights of man, but they would always side with settlers and send the Indians westwards.

Any chance of success was wrecked by Tecumseh's brother, 'the Prophet', who prematurely attacked General Henry Harrison, Governor of Indiana Territory at Tippicanoe, instead of waiting for Tecumseh. Harrison's victory gained him the Presidency years later.

That disastrous battle was fought in 1811, spelling doom to Tecumseh's cause. In 1812, he sided with the British, who were delighted to have such an ally, but the following year he was killed at the Battle of the Thames. His body was spirited away and rumours of his survival swept the Frontier. Meanwhile, the impossible dream of Indian unity died forever.

Small reservations remained – and remain – in the East, but basically Indian Removal was total. When Black Hawk's War in 1832 was over and his tribe driven to Iowa, the North was virtually 'free' of Indians. It was – and more notoriously – almost over in the South as well.

The Five Civilized Tribes

Of all the enforced removals, the most famous of an infamous succession of them was the banishing of the Five Civilized Tribes – the Cherokee, Creek, Choctaw, Chickasaw, and Seminole – from the South. Once renowned for their ferocity, they had made remarkable progress, especially the Cherokee, who swiftly became literate after Sequoyah's invention of a Cherokee alphabet. There was a

Cherokee newspaper by 1828. Meanwhile, in the 1790s, the Creek halfblood leader, Alexander McGillivray, proved a master not of the battlefield but of diplomacy, speaking six languages and showing cunning and wisdom in his dealings with Britain, Spain and the United States. He died in 1796, when the Seminole were part of the Creek Nation.

Many members of the tribes had served Andrew Jackson well in their time, but that did not help them when that notable Indian-hater became President in 1828. Georgia – whose 'poor whites' lived far less well than the Cherokee – Mississippi and Alabama were eager to help Jackson, the Georgians even more so when gold was found in the state. Chief Justice John Marshall stated that Georgia had no right to Cherokee lands, to which Jackson made his infamous reply: 'John Marshall has made his decision; now let him enforce it.'

A sympathetic citizen of Maine was later to describe the Cherokee on their Trail of Tears towards Indian Territory:

When I passed the last detachment of those suffering exiles and thought that my native countrymen had thus expelled them from their native soil and their much loved homes, and that too in this inclement season of the year, I turned from the sight with feelings which language cannot express and 'wept like childhood then'.

Naturally, the actual cruelty of these trails varied, many soldiers hating their task, but overall they disgraced the nation. These Indians were decent citizens from areas that had long been peaceful, but they were 'different', prosperous – and doomed.

The Seminole were the only tribe able to resist because their chosen location, the Florida Everglades, was almost impregnable. Almost but not quite, for there was always treachery. The First Seminole War had been fought from 1816–18 when Spain ruled Florida. Runaway Black slaves had fled to shelter with the tribe and Jackson followed them and defeated the Seminole. Soon Florida joined the Union. The second war, from 1835–42, was very different, an Indian epic and a taste of hell for Amecian soldiers. The great Seminole leader Osceola survived attacks by troops and bloodhounds, but was seized under a flag of truce, and died in prison.

Right: Troops in 1839 in Florida during the Second Seminole War, with an Indian scout.

Far right: John Ross, the part Scottish Cherokee leader, who led his people on the Trail of Tears from Georgia to Indian Territory in what is now Oklahoma.

Below: In the war of 1812 Tecumseh, the great Shawnee, allied himself with the British. He was killed at the Battle of the Thames in Canada in 1813.

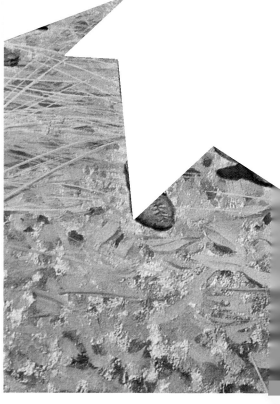

Another leading Seminole was Wild Cat. With 16 warriors and two women he led a sensational escape from Fort Marion through a small hole 18 feet (5.5 m) from the ground in a wall of the fort. So ferociously determined were the Seminole that mothers in the Everglades were prepared to kill their children so that they could fight alongside the warriors.

In the end, the Americans gave in. Those of the tribe who wanted to remain in Florida were allowed to do so. In 1962, they finally resumed relations with the United States.

One of those who fought the Seminoles, General Jessop, had this to say:

If the war be carried on it must necessarily be one of extermination. We have, at no former period in our history, had to contend with so formidable an enemy. No Seminole proves false to his country, nor has a single instance ever occurred of a first rate warrior having surrendered.

The Seminole are not the only members of the five tribes to have representatives in the East. On one of the many Trails of Tears, some few hundred Cherokee escaped and hid in the North Carolina hills. Today, their descendants number some 4,500. Unlike the Cherokee of Oklahoma they have not intermarried with other groups, and every year visitors to their beautiful reservation can enjoy the most famous of all Indian dramas about a tribe's past, *Unto These Hills*. It is a happy note on which to end a tragic chapter.

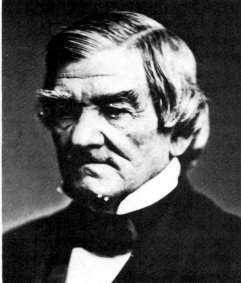

CHAPTER FIVE

LEWIS AND CLARK

Like George Washington, Thomas Jefferson believed in westward expansion. Back in 1793, a resolute Scottish fur trader, Alexander Mackenzie, had reached the Pacific overland through the Canadian wilderness, but no Americans followed his example further south. Then, in 1801, President Jefferson learnt that Napoleon had made a secret treaty with Spain that gave Louisiana back to France, which she had lost in 1763.

The territory included not just the modern state, but the 800,000 square miles between the Mississippi and the Rockies. Francophile as Jefferson was, the idea of a Napoleonic army in New Orleans alarmed him to the extent that he felt Americans 'must marry ourselves to the British fleet and nation'. It was clear that the great port must be fought for or bought, preferably the latter. Fortunately for the United States, the French lost so many troops in the West Indies from disease and slave uprisings, that Napoleon, his mind on Mediterranean conquests, decided to sell. The astonished Americans got far more than they expected, the whole Louisiana Purchase, as it was called, costing them a mere 15 million dollars. Though his political enemies called Jefferson's deal the 'wildest chimera of a moonstruck brain', it was undoubtedly the best land transaction in history.

Being the man he was, Jefferson wanted it explored at once. An expedition was organized, the leaders being Captain Meriwether Lewis, who was Jefferson's secretary, and Lieutenant William Clark, brother of the great George Rogers Clark. They were ordered to explore the Missouri River and, if possible, find a water route to the Pacific, as well as to study the

Left: Meriwether Lewis. He died in 1809 not long after his triumphant expedition. Some believed he killed himself, others that he was murdered.

Below: William Clark. After his epic journey he became Superintendant of Indian Affairs and was much regarded and liked by Indians.

Indian tribes they encountered and the flora and fauna along the route.

Though an awesome adventure for the 30 or so members of the expedition who completed the whole trip, in retrospect it was a peaceful start to a story that is often and with reason summed up in the two words 'Wild West'. A single Blackfoot killed and another wounded was to cause years of trouble with that tribe, but generally relations with the Indians were excellent and a great deal of informa-tion about the tribes was brought back.

The party started up the Missouri on May 14th, 1804. On August 20th it suffered its only casualty, Sergeant Charles Floyd dying of 'bilious colic' — possibly a fatal attack of appendicitis. There were only two major disciplin-ary problems. The first was the deser-tion of Moses Reed, who was found among the Oto Indians and punished by running the gauntlet four times while the men beat him with 'swichies'; the second was the flog-ging and discharging of Private John Newman for malingering. The flog-ging upset an Indian chief who saw it, and told Clark that his own people were never whipped. So what would the chief have done, Clark enquired? Kill the man, replied the chief.

The expedition spent the winter with the Mandan Indians at what is now Bismarck, North Dakota, the nearest they had come to real danger being from potentially hostile Teton Sioux. From the Mandans they learnt that the Missouri was navigable al-most to its source and that not half a day's march away they would find a river running from South to North. 'We believe this stream to be the principal south fork of the Columbia River', wrote Clark, who knew that it would lead the expedition to the sea.

It was during the winter that a key member was added to the expedition, the Shoshoni girl Sacajawea. She had been captured some years before by the Minnetaree, who sold her to a French Canadian named Toussaint Charbonneau, as wretched a character as she was admirable. She was now married to him and became pregnant, giving birth to a boy, whom she was to carry on her back while guiding the party and acting as an interpreter. Just how much Sacajawea contributed to the expedition's success has been disputed, but assist it she did, not least because the sight of her with a baby on her back helped show watching Indi-ans that the expedition was a peaceful one.

Other interesting characters on the journey were Clark's slave York, later freed by his master. He was particu-larly popular with some of the Indian girls met along the way. Lewis also had his giant Northumberland dog

Scannon with him and he, too, was widely admired.

When they had crossed the Continental Divide and were on the Pacific slope, it became vital to replace their boats with horses. Sacajawea, who had been becoming steadily more useful as a guide the nearer she got to home, now made a decisive contribution. Her people, the Shoshoni, seemed unfriendly at first, then the girl recognized the chief, her brother, and horses were soon made available. Sacajawea and her family stayed with the expedition as it pushed on towards the Pacific.

The mouth of the Columbia was reached in November 1805, Pacific breakers being heard on the 7th. The men built a fort for the winter, the Pacific hardly living up to its name, and it must have come as a great relief when the journey home began on March 23rd, 1806. Apart from the incident with the Blackfoot, the worst thing that happened was the shooting by a one-eyed man of the unfortunate Lewis in the buttocks, the culprit having mistaken him for an elk or a bear.

Lewis, Clark and their men reached St. Louis on September 23rd, 1806, to the delight of many who had feared them dead. The knowledge they had gained — geographical, botanical and zoological — was extensive and all of it carefully documented. A mass of information had also been gained about the Indians, relations between the races being as friendly on the whole as they were later to be so lamentable. The journals of Lewis and of Clark are among the classics of exploration.

Lewis became Governor of Louisi-

Left: Charles Russell's painting of Indians discovering Lewis and Clark.

Left: Sacajawea guiding Lewis and Clark in this picture by E.S. Paxon.

Right: Lewis and Clark on the Columbia River, painted by Harold von Schmidt.

Below: These woodcuts formed part of the first published account of the Lewis and Clark Expedition.

ana Territory, but in 1809, on his way to Washington, he died in an isolated cabin in Tennessee. Jefferson, thinking that Lewis had been upset by certain criticisms levelled against his financial accounts, believed that he had committed suicide, but it is generally thought that he was murdered for his money. Lewis was a moody, solitary man, and his friend Clark also thought at first that he might have killed himself. Later he was to deny the possibility. He died in 1838. He had had Sacajawea's three children educated and was one of the few whites of his day whom the Indians venerated and loved.

As for Sacajawea, there is little doubt that she died of a 'putrid fever' at Fort Manuel in what is now South Dakota in 1812. Years later, Dr. Grace Hebard, State Historian of Wyoming, convinced herself that Sacajawea lived on until 1884 when she died on the Shohshonis' Wind River Reservation in Wyoming. This must rank as the greatest discrepancy ever in the date of death of an important person, but most experts are convinced that she did indeed die sadly young. A clerk at the fort recorded her death briefly but movingly—'. . . this Evening the wife of Charbonneau, a Snake squaw, died of a putrid fever. She was a good and the best woman in the fort.'

CHAPTER SIX
THE MOUNTAIN MEN

Some were from Missouri and Kentucky, others were French-Canadians and Mexicans. There were Blacks amongst them. They wore what Le-Roy Hafen has described as perhaps the only original American costume – the fringed buckskin suit. Their finest contemporary historian and most vivid chronicler was Frederick Ruxton, late of the British Eighty-Ninth Regiment, whose *Life in the Far West* remains one of the few outright classics of the West. They were virtually white Indians and they have come down to us as the Mountain Men.

No tougher white men ever roamed the West. Their job was to trap beaver, the fur being fashionable in the East and in Europe from around 1810 to the end of the 1830s. Carrying out their work they blazed trails all over the West, trails that would later be used by other, less legendary mortals. The story of the Mountain Men is part fact, part romance, part epic in the vein of the *Iliad* and *Beowulf*. When silk hats replaced beaver ones and the fur trade rapidly declined, these wild men – those who survived – could only hope to guide wagon trains or scout. Farming for them was an impossibility.

The first Western Mountain Man is often considered to have been John Colter, one of Lewis and Clark's men. Of course 'Mountain' is a misleading, if satisfying, word, for these men were equally at home on the Plains and in deserts as well. All of the West was their territory.

Colter was the first white man to see the soaring Tetons of Wyoming and the marvels of Yellowstone. He is chiefly remembered, however, for a race against death, which, like so many

Mountain Men epics, cannot be guaranteed to be completely true, but which there is no reason to doubt.

One autumn day in 1808, he was captured by Blackfoot in Montana

Above: A Trapper crossing the Mountains *by William T. Ranney. Mountain Men were the chief trailblazers of the West.*

46

after a fellow trapper named John Potts had been killed by them. The tall Virginian was stripped naked and the Indians discussed what to do with him. It was now that Colter was to suffer because of the Blackfoot killed during the Lewis and Clark expedition, even though that brave had been trying to steal rifles. Possibly the Indian who had been wounded was present that day as well. So Colter was a victim of the feud, his position made worse because he had fought with the Crow against the Blackfoot not long before.

A chief asked Colter how fast a runner he was. He was, in fact, very fast, but declared that he was as slow as a turtle. This encouraged the Blackfoot to tell him to run for his life. They would be after him in about half a minutes time.

He raced away towards the Jefferson fork of the Madison River, thorns and prickly pear tearing at his feet. Three miles or so on he had outstripped all his pursuers except one. He suddenly turned on the brave and killed him with his own spear after tripping him. Then he ran on.

Reaching the river, he plunged in, swam to some driftwood and hid underneath it as the runners came into view. They scoured the bank for him, then gave up with howls of rage.

He swam downstream, came ashore and started running again. After a week-long nightmare journey, living through freezing nights and burning days, his feet bloody lumps of flesh, his food chiefly roots, he reached his camp on the Bighorn River. He was now an awesome sight, even by Mountain Man standards, but he soon recovered from his ordeal. Only death could deter the Mountain Man.

Giants of the Fur Trade

The businessmen who ran the fur trade were in their way as outsize characters as the men they employed. John Jacob Astor, founder of a famous family, started out as a poor German immigrant. Back in the East he carried stinking furs out of the Indian country, so beginning his rise to staggering riches. In the 1790s, he had discovered that beaver skin could be bought from an Indian for a piece

of cheap, bright cloth, then sold at a 900 percent gain.

He was up against two great Canadian companies, the old Hudson's Bay Company – the H.B.C., 'Here Before

Above: Jim Baker, a famous Mountain Man and army scout. Naturally Mountain Men also crossed plains and deserts, too.

47

Above: Unlike most Mountain Men Jedediah Smith, who was also a great trailblazer, was a quiet, sober Bible-reader.

Left: Fur Traders descending the Missouri *painted by George Caleb Bingham.*

Christ' – and the North West Company, with which it amalgamated in 1821. Astor's first fortune having been made in the East, he dreamed of building a western empire based on 'Astoria', which was to be erected on the Pacific Coast at the mouth of the Columbia River. There would be a chain of similar posts and forts eastwards to the Missouri. In the event, bad management together with bad luck ruined his plans, and the disappointed Astor concentrated on his main company. He once sold 500,000 muskrat skins in a single day, and when he foresaw the end of beaver skin as high fashion, he got out in time and concentrated on property.

The true fur trade kings of the West were a Spaniard and two Americans. Manuel Lisa, realizing that the fur trade in the West could not depend on Indians bringing pelts to the whites, as in the East, because the Western Indians were mounted and preferred hunting buffalo to trapping beaver, hired his own trappers. Colter was one of the first.

The American 'kings' were William Ashley and Andrew Henry who often led their own expeditions. Two of their men in particular were to prove able leaders, Jedediah Smith and Jim Bridger. As for Lisa, until he died in 1820, he had the Missouri trade under tight control, and, businessman as he was, he could address hundreds of hostile Indians and, if he had to, fight them.

Two years after his death, Ashley and Henry inserted a famous advertisement in several Missouri papers. One in the *Missouri Republican* for March 20th, 1822 read as follows:

TO ENTERPRISING YOUNG MEN

The subscriber wishes to engage one hundred young men to as-

cend the Missouri River to its source, there to be employed for one, two, or three years. For particulars enquire of Major Andrew Henry, near the lead mines in the County of Washington, who will ascend with, and command, the party; or the subscriber near St. Louis.

(Signed) WILLIAM H. ASHLEY

The following year another advertisement was inserted, and the two together brought forth a galaxy of legendary figures to be – Tom 'Broken Hand' Fitzpatrick, Jim Bridger, Jedediah Smith, an ex-Mississippi pirate and bandit, Edward Rose, who was a Cherokee-Negro, James Clyman, the Sublette Brothers, and Hugh Glass, whose most legendary adventure cannot be left out of this chapter even if it is – legend!

Young Jim Bridger could not read, but someone read the exciting advertisement to him. It was a call that would bring the era of the Mountain Man to its climax.

British influence was such in what Americans now considered their Northwest that Ashley and Henry had to combat it, though, in fact, Indians were to prove the chief problem during the first expeditions. The pair founded the Rocky Mountain Fur Company, but by 1824, Henry had had enough and returned to the East, leaving Ashley to lead his men on many a rugged trek. When their time with Ashley ended, some Mountain Men hired out their skills, others worked solo or in small groups. All of them fought Indians; most of them married them.

Tough as they were, not all Mountain Men were wild. 'Jed' Smith, one of the very greatest of them, was both sober and religious. He it was who pioneered the route to California, leading a group across the deserts of southern Nevada and eastern California. He was to experience even worse treks – Mountain Men were the first and most important white trailblazers of the West – and he survived a savage mauling from a grizzly bear and many

Above: Fort Laramie as it was in 1837, when it was a fur trading post, the artist being Alfred J. Miller.

Right: Jim Beckwourth was a mulatto from Virginia whose amazing adventures included becoming a Crow chief.

an Indian fight before a Comanche lance killed him in 1831. He was only thirty-one.

Fact and fiction are impossibly mixed in the epic of the Mountain Men, not least because they enjoyed telling tall stories even more than most Westerners. Jim Beckwourth's autobiography, as told to Thomas D. Bonner, hopelessly divides expert opinion, though by any standard, the Virginian-born mulatto who became a Crow chief had an amazing life. Trouble starts on page one, for, as its modern editor, Delmont Oswald asks, on which side in the Revolution was Beckwourth's white major father, the Rebel or the Loyalist?

Jim Bridger's life is less controversial. He was an illiterate who could speak French and ten Indian languages. He survived countless Indian fights and was the first white man to sample the bitter waters of the Great Salt Lake. After the collapse of the fur trade, he lived another four decades, working as a trader, a guide and a scout. No white man can have ever known the West better than he, one of his memory aids being to turn and look *back* regularly on the trail, not just sideways and forwards. Like many a Westerner, he dry-cleaned his buckskins over an ant hill. He, too, told tall stories, the tallest-seeming often being true.

As for Old Hugh Glass, the most famous story about him should not be written off as myth. He was deserted by two companions after coming off second best in a fight with a grizzly. Enraged at being abandoned, he set off to seek revenge. On his 200-mile crawl he lived on berries and the bodies of dead buffalo calves.

The first of the two deserters he found was Jim Bridger, or so many accounts have it. Bridger's leading biographer, J. Cecil Alter, convincingly has it otherwise. The old man forgave whoever it was, but kept up the search for the other culprit, finally running him down only to find that as he was in the Army he could not be touched.

On the Canadian side of the border, there were heroes as well, most notably Pete Skene Ogden of Hudson's Bay Company. International politics finally beat the Company's leaders in the Northwest – John McLoughlin, who helped many Americans on the Oregon Trail, and Sir George Simpson – for in 1846, the Oregon Treaty gave the United States the Oregon country and the 49th Parallel became the final boundary line.

The annual highspot of a Mountain Man's life was the rendezvous camp. The camp had been Ashley's idea and was often in the Rockies. Agents from the fur companies came to the rendezvous with money, weapons, tools and other goods that were exchanged for skins. Mountain Men tended to be such dedicated gamblers that they often staked their entire earnings in a single crazy spree. However, as money meant almost as little to them as it did to their Indian friends and enemies, it hardly mattered. Settling down was not their objective.

The gatherings were wild affairs, the days filled with drinking, talking, trading, horse-racing and the inevitable gambling, as well as finding themselves Indian wives. Battles were fought, not all of them in jest, while at night the camp rang with singing, drunken roars and great gusts of laughter.

As the 1830s progressed these annual meetings steadily grew smaller. Veterans like Old Bill Williams and newcomers to the fur trade like Kit Carson were forced to realise that the old way of life would collapse with the

fur trade. In fact, the beaver population of the West was almost extinct from over-trapping, though the trade survived in Canada.

Few Mountain Men, as said, could bear the thought of farming, most veterans of the trade becoming guides to explorers or wagon trains. Besides, the West in the 1840s was still the violent, beautiful paradise that Mountain Men had grown to love.

Some remained in the wilderness because it was just that, while some arrived late. Such a one was John Johnston, whose life – in somewhat watered-down form – inspired one of the few worthy films about Mountain Men, *Jeremiah Johnson*.

The real Johnson, who lost the 't' in his name as time went on, was known as 'Liver-Eating' Johnson. In 1847, Crow Indians killed his pregnant wife, then scalped her, after which he began a personal war against the tribe, killing and scalping them – and eating their livers. What makes the story epic rather than horrifying is that the last of his victims, 20 in all, came at him one by one. And after he had purged himself of his hatred of the Crow, he became their friend.

CHAPTER SEVEN

WESTWARD THE WAGONS

Night and day, the uproar never ceased. Whips, cracked, wagons creaked, shouts and raucous laughter split the air; but above the din there was the never-ending sound of hammers on anvils in a score of blacksmiths' shops. In them, the covered wagons were being repaired and readied for the 2,000-mile journey to Oregon.

The place was Independence, Missouri, its streets crowded with oxen, mules and horses, and men who ranged from trappers and Indians and Spanish traders to gamblers and storekeepers. But the largest group were the emigrants, the men, women and children who were ready to finish what their grandparents had begun beyond the Appalachians – the colonizing of the continent. The time was the early 1840s and once again America was on the move.

Independence had some 30 stores, two hotels, many boarding houses and some 1,600 inhabitants in 1843. It marked the start of three great trails, the Santa Fe, the California and the Oregon. The first had been operating since the 1820s, as a trading, not an emigrant, trail, the California being a modest one until gold was found in 1848. The Oregon, though less used than the post-gold strike California, was *the* trail.

Early visitors to Oregon discovered a fertile land, ripe for settlement. They included the Reverend Jason Lee, who had set up a small mission in the Willamette Valley. On his return East, he lectured to enthralled thousands, many of whom must have believed that the valley was like the promised land and paradise rolled into one.

Politicians and newspapers, meanwhile, took up the call, for, as we have seen, Britain and the USA were dis-

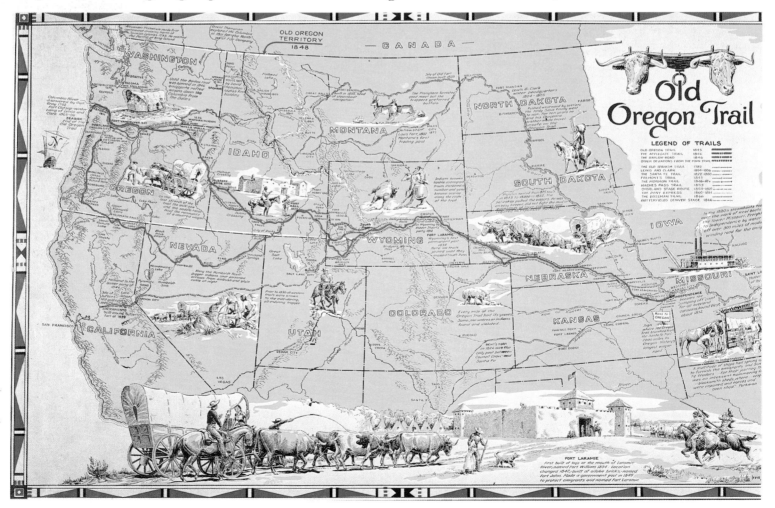

Left: The great 2,000 mile trail to Oregon. The cut-off trail to California really came into its own after gold had been discovered there.

puting the ownership of Oregon, an undramatic sounding quarrel called the Oregon Question. The American point of view was that if enough settlers could reach the disputed area, the Oregon country would be indeed American. So the trumpet call became part crusade, part wanderlust and part land hunger – a heady mixture.

Though the first emigrants crossed in 1841, it was the 'Great Emigration' of 1843 that set the pattern for the future and solved the 'Question'. The 1846 treaty confirmed the matter and the boundary, as noted, became the 49th Parallel. In fact, only some 10,000 reached Oregon in the 1840s, but it was they who changed history in a trek that tested human endurance to the limit.

In May 1843, some 200 families and others, about 1,000 in all, gathered on the Missouri frontier. Congress had offered 640 acres to every male reach-

ing Oregon, 160 for his wife and 160 for each child. May 18th was rendez-vous day, some miles from Independence, and the start would be as soon as possible for Oregon had to be reached before the winter.

Though a few wagons were elaborate, most were farm wagons, some ten feet long by four feet. Few family treasures could be taken. Buckets were often hung under the carts together with a churn, lanterns, farming tools and water kegs, while inside were pots and pans, baskets, clothing and rifles. Bedding had to fit on the over-crowded floor, though many used tents.

Oxen were used as a rule once it was realized how much stronger and more reliable they were than horses or mules. The wagons wound their way through the settlements, rendezvous-bound, women and children walking alongside. Veteran Mountain Man

John Gantt was elected pilot, together with a captain and a council of ten. There was a delay in 1843 because a late spring had kept the grass too short for the stock, then, on May 22nd, they were off.

The first night out was a time of singing and laughter. Later, the elected captain, Peter Burnett, was to write: 'Our long journey began in sunshine and song, in anecdote and laughter: but these all vanished before we had reached its termination.'

There was luck at the start when medical missionary Dr. Marcus Whitman, who had first been in Oregon in 1836 – with a colleague and their wives – joined the party and was able to help its leaders. Over the years, the average train travelled 2 miles an hour and 12 miles a day. If a wagon broke down, its occupants often had to be left behind because of the fear of the oncoming winter. That was far from most people's minds in the idyllic days in eastern Kansas. Forty miles from Independence the trail to Santa Fe began, while a magical sign proclaimed the road to Oregon.

Wagons were put in a circle each afternoon as protection against Indians, for pitching camp took time, yet they never attacked a train in the 1840s. That came later with the mass exodus to California, racial tensions and hatreds, land grabbing and atrocities on each side. In fact, Indians were as loath to attack a circle of wagons as they were to launch a frontal assault on a stockaded fort. Both were foolish tactics, though both happen in innumerable Westerns.

The real enemies on the trail were terrain, outbreaks of cholera, constant diarrhoea and sheer strain. As for the dreaded winter, the California Trail was to provide the classic horror story of that. In 1846 the Donner Party was trapped in the Sierra Nevada and were forced to cannibalism, seven men and a boy being eaten in a makeshift camp

after they had died, some while their families looked on.

Fuel, at least, was no problem on the Plains, dried buffalo dung known as 'buffalo chips' being used. In the 1843 crossing there was a 'Cow Column' 5,000 strong, those who had no cattle resenting having to help look after it. Finally, the party was split, the Cow Column travelling in the rear.

The day began at 4 am and anyone not ready to move by 7 am was likely to 'eat dust' at the rear of the column. A halt was made at noon, and in the evening stragglers could catch up.

Crossing the Platte was a great event. Described by one wit as 'too

Above: Where Wagon Trails Were Dim *by Charles Russell.*

Left: A properly unromantic photograph of weary-looking pioneers nearing the Rockies.

thick to drink and too thin to plough', Mark Twain was to say it was a mile wide and an inch deep. In fact, it was much deeper and could be mean and treacherous. It split into two at its forks in Nebraska. The 1843 travellers learnt to turn their wagons into boats, covering the box tops by sewing together buffalo hides and stretching them across the top. The sun dried the skins and made a raft for all except the man of a party, who walked alongside.

It could be perilous, as Jesse Applegate recalled more than half a century later, looking back on his crossing at the age of seven. Some drowned in deep patches and the boy never forgot how the water overflowed into the wagon boxes, and how it was decided to chain all the wagons together in a single file.

On July 14th, Fort Laramie was reached, where, during the two-day stay the women could have their first wash day since the start. After Laramie the going got steadily worse. Signatures were scratched on Independence Rock, but now the trail down the year would contain more and more broken wheels and utensils, mouldering scaffolds for drying meat – and graves.

The Trail led through South Pass in the Rockies and the emigrants were over the backbone of the continent. The 1843 party headed southwest to trade at Fort Bridger, run by the great man himself. Others would head

directly across a waterless 50-mile stretch, where many humans and animals would die. The two trails linked up again on the way to the Hudson's Bay Company post at Fort Hall.

Soda Springs was the main separation point for the California Trail, but in 1843 it was 'Oregon – or bust!' The front of the wagon train reached Fort Hall on August 27th and all were advised to sell their wagons and proceed by horse, at which moment Dr. Whitman appeared. He urged them to keep their wagons, get to the Columbia and float downstream on rafts. His fervour convinced them, though they had to cross the Snake river twice.

The terrain killed off some of the valiant oxen. 'We could see our faithful oxen dying inch by inch', one traveller later wrote. The Devil's Backbone was an awesome ordeal, with a gorge on the left and the Snake far below on the right – and just enough width for the wagons, with not a foot to spare. Everyone walked.

After some 1,700 miles, the great expedition split up. The Walla Walla River flowed into the Columbia and some who could not bear to part with their wagons forced them along the almost impassible south bank of the Columbia. Later, they built rafts and landed again near the ominously named Cascades, local Indians carrying their belongings around the rapids. Finally, they reached Fort Vancouver in what would become Washington State. Soon, they were crossing the Columbia in small groups and heading down the Willhamette to settle, helped by those who had come before.

The other members of the expedition had a tougher time. There were some 200 miles to be travelled from Fort Walla Walla and the men built 'skiffs' for the journey from drift wood. Leaving their cattle and wag-

Left: The interior of the first Fort Laramie in 1837, painted by Alfred Jacob Miller, who travelled West with a Scottish adventurer, Sir William Drummond Stewart.

ons at the fort, they set off down the Columbia. The Applegate family suffered cruelly on that nightmare journey, Jesse watching a boat strike a rock, upturning and flinging its six occupants into the foam. He lost a young cousin in the tragedy.

Finally, in small flotillas, the emigrants reached Fort Vancouver to be lent tools and seed by the Hudson's Bay Company's famous official, John McLoughlin, whose reign would soon be over. The emigrants, as earlier ones had and later ones would do, settled in the lovely wilderness. The ruts that their wagon wheels had made can be seen in places to this day.

There will be more about the California Trail in the next chapter. Meanwhile, as traffic on the Oregon Trail was reaching its peak, events in the East were conspiring to set up a trail that was so different that it ranks as unique.

Mormon Saga

This was the Mormon Trail. Whereas most who headed westwards hoped for a better life, meaning land or gold, and some for adventure or to escape the law, the Mormons sought religious freedom. Whatever some felt about their life-style and beliefs, none of those who knew of their achievements could deny their magnificent spirit.

Their first leader, Joseph Smith, founded his Church of Jesus Christ of Latter Day Saints in New York State in 1830. He produced the Book of Mormon as his church's bible. He and his flock were driven from their first home in Ohio because the neighbours objected. This was to happen regularly. The hard-working but narrow sect came to Missouri and their success, plus the fact that they were staunchly anti-slavery in a slave area, led to riots and flight to Illinois. On the Mississippi, they founded Nauvoo.

Smith, an arrogant man, considered himself above local law. In 1843, he announced that polygamy was permitted, which not only split the Mormons but outraged the local 'Gentiles'. A mob set upon him and killed him.

A remarkable man, Brigham Young, took his place, a masterful 43-year-old who, in mid-winter, led his people to temporary safety in 'Camp of Israel', then, the next winter, to 'Winter Quarters' in Nebraska.

In the following spring of 1847, a

Above: A Mormon wagon train bound for Salt Lake City, photographed in Echo Canyon in 1867.

Left: The Oregon Trail by Alfred Bierstadt.

Right: A Mormon husband surrounded by his wives and children.

tightly-disciplined advance party started out under Young and came to Salt Lake City. Smith said simply: 'This is the place' and crops were being planted the following day.

The fervent Mormons were saved by a veritable miracle the next spring, by which time thousands more had or were trekking to Salt Lake. Millions of grasshoppers, which became known as Mormon Crickets, descended on the young wheat and began eating it. When all seemed utterly lost, seagulls saved the day by devouring the grasshoppers. The seagull is now an honoured bird in Salt Lake City.

Armies of recruits were soon crossing the Plains, many from as far afield as Britain, where converts were made in the industrial slums. The Mormons had a genius for attracting disciples.

Young's historic idea for 1849 was handcarts! These were to carry baggage of up to 500 lb (227 kg). Over four years, some 3,000 Saints pulled their carts to Salt Lake City. They averaged 30 miles a day, more than twice as fast as the average oxen-teams achieved.

Mormons, for all that they 'made the desert bloom', still attracted hostility, polygamy seeming infinitely more immoral than other aspects of Western life. Besides, there was something odd about people who were not interested in gold. Brigham Young said it was for paving streets.

Young was made Territorial Governor of Utah in 1850, but tensions between 'Gentiles' and Mormons continued. Their cause was not helped when some Mormons and Utes wiped out a band of some undeniably troublesome emigrants. President Buchanan declared Utah to be in a state of armed rebellion. It had been no fault of Brigham Young's. This extraordinary leader died in 1877,

Right: The Rocky Mountains: Immigrants crossing the Plains — *a lithograph by Currier and Ives, suitably romanticized.*

leaving $2 million to his 17 wives and 56 children. Nineteen years later, with polygamy officially abolished, Mormon and Gentile were brought together when Utah became a state.

'Remember the Alamo!'

In 1821, Mexico broke free from Spain, and that very year 300 American families settled in Texas with the blessing of the new government. They were led by a 28-year-old, flute-playing lawyer named Stephen Austin, who was as quiet a personality as the traditional Texan has been flamboyant.

From the outset, the Anglo-American settlers, whose traditions and customs were so different from Spanish ones, riled the government in Mexico City. The Mexicans had abolished slavery, but the colonists had brought their slaves with them from the South. Mexican motives, considering the treatment handed out to their own unfortunate peasants, may not have been so much a rush of liberalism to the head as a shot at the cotton economy of the newcomers. Austin persuaded the Government to agree that the children of slaves should be freed at 14 and that no slave could be sold after coming to Texas. For the moment crisis was averted.

It erupted again in 1833, when the

Right: The great Sam Houston, painted by L. Markos.

Below: The storming of the Alamo, with Santa Anna urging on his men. Later, avenging Texans would use 'Remember the Alamo!' as their battle-cry.

dictator Santa Anna became President of Mexico after a coup. There were now 20,000 Anglo-Americans in Texas and at first many welcomed the newcomer as a man who might govern well and grant them privileges. Alas, Santa Anna, elegant, proud and cruel, and so refined that he used a silver chamber pot on his campaigns, proved no friend. The Texans prepared to rebel.

The year of decision was 1836, with the American Texans by this time outnumbering local Mexicans by some 30,000 to 7,000.

Naturally, things went well for the Texans at first, but General Santa Anna, his pride and ruthlessness making him a menacing enemy, was heading northwards, bent on punishment.

Texas had declared herself independent at Washington-on-the-Brazos, its army being put under the command of the remarkable Sam Houston, although he had not fought since the Creek War of 1814. He had been Governor of Tennessee and a Congressman, and had a notable reputation as a drinker. He had also lived with the Cherokee, and indeed was that rarest of beings, a Texan who genuinely loved Indians. He was a likeable, brilliant man.

Meanwhile, Santa Anna was closing in on a mission hastily turned into a fortress called the Alamo. It was to be defended from February 23rd to March 6th, 1836 by men whose heroism remains inspirational – some 180

Union. The rest was acquired in 1853. As we shall see in the next chapter, the peace treaty came at a most fortunate time because of events in California.

Peopling the Plains

The Anglo-American frontiersmen who explored the Great Plains, with their unlimited grasslands and lack of timber, and the sun burning down on the soil, did not consider the area as farming land. So unimpressed were they by its possibilities that they were responsible for the start of the myth of the Great American Desert. The myth even got onto maps, and the Homestead Act of 1862, which gave 160 acres (64.8 hectares) of land to any adult citizen for a $10 fee, and the opportunity of being granted the final title five years later, cannot have seemed quite as good a bargain as it was meant to be. In fact, what really weakened the bargain was lack of the fee by many, lack of money for the move, lack of the correct farming experience, and lack of funds to keep going in the early days.

Worse than these handicaps for the pioneer, who was meant to be given a promising start, were the activities of land speculators, cattlemen, lumber interests and others who used this and later acts to secure more and more land by questionable means. In addition there was the general lawlessness summed up in the phrase 'Wild West'. Yet despite every handicap, between 1860 and 1900, eleven new Western states were admitted to the Union.

The human beings who made that possible dispelled the 'Desert' myth. The ground might be harder to cultivate than Oregon's, but from their earth and grass sod houses, the 'sodbusters' went out to make a livelihood. Neither the elements nor human enemies could deter them, though the cost in human terms was great, especially for the women. In Cora Beach's *Women of Wyoming*, a Wyoming woman, Mrs Henry Gray, recalled how she had 'fought bedbugs and flies all summer, scrubbed rough plank floors and mingled my tears with the suds'.

The stark loneliness could become unendurable. Nervous breakdowns were common, some women went mad. One pioneer remembered that when his father went seven miles for the mail, 'Mother cried until he returned. She was afraid that he would be killed.' Another pioneer wife, this time in Montana, was to recall that there was 'nothing a woman left alone on a ranch can't imagine when she is afraid'. It was the old nightmare that had haunted generations of pioneer women and their husbands, for nightmares could so easily come true on the successive frontiers.

Women were expected to help with the ploughing as well as tend the garden, if there was one. They could handle wagons and plant seeds, and with the nearest doctor often more than 50 miles away they had to try and keep the family fit. Warmed up urine was a standard cure for earache. As for prairie fires, storms, drought, blizzards, locusts, tornadoes, these were part of daily life.

The shortage of women in the post-Civil War West was not as serious as in Gold Rush California, but the sheer size of the West saw to it that at many a ranch house dance most of the 'female' dancers were 'heifer-branded' cowboys. A sodbuster's daughter could be a link between those traditional enemies, the farmer and the cowboy.

A trip to 'town' – anything from a booming frontier community to a few shacks in the wilderness – as immortalized romantically in *Shane* – was always an event for pioneer families. As well as all the more lurid happenings which have been so exploited down the years – and around the world – in Western films, there was a remarkable amount of culture to be found, not all of it of a makeshift nature. Grand opera companies, some from Europe, crossed the West in special trains, as did theatrical troupes. Sarah Bernhardt, Edwin Booth, Adelina Patti and a host of other superstars of their day were among those who performed in the West. Cheyenne, a wild end-of-track in the

Right: A New Mexican family, photographed about 1895. Note the Indian servant-nurse.

Below: Runnymede Tennis Club in Kansas. In the late 1880s Runnymede was virtually a little piece of England – middle and upper class England – in the West. Alas, despite much fun, this English venture collapsed.

70

late 1860s, was playing host to a Covent Garden opera company in 1885, *La Sonnambula* being presented at the Opera House. The manager of the company, Colonel Mapleson, noted:

To my astonishment, although Cheyenne is but a little town, consisting of about two streets, it possesses a most refined society, composed, it is true, of cowboys; yet one might have imagined one's self at the London Opera when the curtain rose – the ladies in brilliant toilettes and covered with diamonds; the gentlemen all in evening dress.

'Cowboys' is perhaps not the right word, for many of that audience would have been local ranchers and their wives – cattle kings who would, a decade later, be planning the Johnson County War from the plush Cheyenne Club. But the fact remains that a century ago much of the American West saw more top-class performers than it does today.

Meanwhile, towns were enlivened in a less exalted way by patent medicinemen, complete with cures for everything from biliousness to baldness, and one enterprising 'painless' dentist hired a band to muffle the anguish of his victims.

Gamblers and conmen were waiting for customers, and a few ordinary Westerners were likely to best them. In cowtowns, the tempo of life increased considerably, as will be seen later, but however much or little the average pioneer saw of towns of any sort, they were not part of their lives. An occasional visit to a town might provide a merciful break in a lonely life – even provide excitement. Yet the true images of the pioneers are the ones that they are remembered by – the covered wagon and the sod house or log hut in the wilderness. Some of their children are alive to this day.

CHAPTER EIGHT
"GOLD! GOLD! GOLD!"

In May 1848, through the streets of the small town of San Francisco, a travel-stained, extrovert Mormon named Sam Brannan paraded up and down shouting, 'Gold! Gold! Gold from the American River!' To prove his claim, he waved a bottle full of gold dust.

Brannan's shouts started half a century of gold rushes. He electrified the 800 or so citizens of San Francisco and by June 'all were off to the mines, some on carts, some on horses, some on crutches, and one went in a litter', so one onlooker was to recall.

That was only the local rush. The immortal Forty-Niners set out the following year, and in 1898, those other gold-seeking immortals, the Klondike Stampeders, were on their way. In the intervening years there was adventure, drama, misery and sudden death, and some men actually made fortunes.

Gold was actually discovered on January 24th, 1848, just over a week before the official peace treaty between Mexico and the United States made California American. Annexation had come about in 1847. It had been the principal object of the war against Mexico. With Oregon Territory already hers, the United States now had a Far West.

The first strike that mattered – for there had been a few small ones earlier in the 1840s which made no stir – occurred on the property of a Swiss emigrant, John Sutter. Fleeing from Europe to avoid creditors, he settled in Mexican-owned California in 1839, enjoying the good life, which included two Hawaiian mistresses and a peaceable Indian work-force. He was running into debt, partly because he was too hospitable, when his partner, James Marshall, struck gold.

Marshall was in charge of building a saw mill, and on the historic day, spotted gold in the tailrace of the almost completed mill. Though all hands were sworn to secrecy, the news inevitably leaked out, but as yet there were only some 14,000 whites in California, many of Spanish descent and not so gold-obsessed as Anglo-Americans. It needed Sam Brannan's vivid display in San Francisco to trigger off the first rush. Meanwhile, Sutter had leased the land around the mill from the local Indians for three years, but he never got the title to it. Squatters invaded his land, his business acumen was not good, and he died in 1880 just when Congress decided finally to reward him adequately. As for Marshall, he was finally granted a state pension in 1872, by which time drink and disappointment had ruined him. His pension was stopped and he died a pauper in 1885. A statue to him was erected which cost $25,000.

Back in May 1848, the first stampede was purely local, and included every ship's crew in San Francisco harbour. First news of the strike did not reach the East until August, by

Above: James Marshall, the man who discovered gold in California in 1848, but who was never properly rewarded.

Right: Swiss born John Sutter on whose land the gold was found that set off the greatest of all gold rushes. Frank Buchser painted him in 1866.

Opposite page: Panning for gold in California in 1849.

which time an idyllic summer on the gold-fields was being enjoyed by eager prospectors – a few hundred in May, some 10,000 by the Fall. The weather was perfect, crime, for the first and last time, was virtually non-existent.

Only some struck it rich at the diggings, but there was so much gold to be had that many found at least a reasonable amount. No wonder that men would pan for gold in freezing water under a blazing sun for hour after hour when the chances of at least some success were so good. And in 'dry' diggings there was gold to be picked out of crevices in rock, as Edward Buffum did with his knife. 'Eureka! Oh how my heart beat!' he wrote later. 'I sat still and looked at it some minutes before I touched it, greedily drinking in the pleasure of gazing upon gold that was in my very grasp . . .

A deserter from the army left us a classic description of the mood of those heady days. 'A frenzy seized my soul,' he wrote. 'Piles of gold rose up before me at every step; thousands of slaves bowed to my beck and call; myriads of fair virgins contended for my love. In short, I had a violent attack of gold fever.' Between July 1848 and the end of 1849 out of 1,290 soldiers in Northern California, 716 had deserted.

Panning remained the basic way to seek gold at 'wet' diggings, the miner swirling 'pay dirt' round his water-filled pan. He swirled it under water, raised it, kept on swirling it and jerked it in and out of the water. As the lighter dirt was washed away, the heavier gold went to the pan's bottom. The rocker, or cradle, a wooden box on rockers plus a handle, made life easier. Pay dirt was piled on a hopper with a perforated base, water was poured on to it and the cradle was rocked. The gold-bearing sediment – if any – was caught on riffles — wooden bars. The 'long tom' and the sluice were extensions of the same principle. Later, machines were to blast jets of water at hillsides, while mines were sunk ever deeper. Yet only panning caught the tiniest particles of gold.

Perhaps $10 million was extracted from the new Eldorado in 1848, the magical time when gold could be left lying unguarded. Not so magical, however, was the dysentery, scurvy and rheumatism, then the heavy winter rains and the ice and snow.

By then, news of the finds had swept the Americas and was reaching Europe. And 1849 would be the year of the immortal Forty-Niners.

It was President Polk's message to Congress on December 5th, 1848, based on reliable information, that triggered off the great Rush of 1849. It included the statement that the mineral wealth of the area drained by the Sacramento and San Joaquin river system would pay for the late Mexican

Below: Panning for gold the hard traditional way. The simple pan ensured that nothing of value was lost.

FOR
CALIFORNIA!
Mutual Protection
Trading & Mining Co.

Having purchased the splendid, Coppered and very fast Sailing

Barque EMMA ISIDORA,

Will leave about the 15th of February. This vessel will be fitted in the very best manner and is one of the fastest sailing vessels that goes from this port.

Each member pays 300 dollars and is entitled to an equal proportion of all profits made by the company either at mining or trading, and holds an equal share of all the property belonging to the company. Experienced men well acquainted with the coast and climate are already engaged as officers of the Company. A rare chance is offered to any wishing a safe investment, good home and Large profits.

This Company is limited to 60 and any wishing to improve this opportunity must make immediate application.

An Experienced Physician will go with the company.

For Freight or Passage apply to 23 State Street, corner of Devonshire, where the list of Passengers may be seen.

JAMES H. PRINCE, Agent,
23 State Street, corner of Devonshire St., Boston.

For further Particulars, see the Constitution.

Propeller Power Presses,
142 Washington St., Boston.

Above: Alas, few Forty-Niners were really suited to life in the mining areas, and a long sea journey, even a peaceful one, was not a good preparation for toils ahead.

War 100 times over! And just days later, actual samples of the gold reached Washington via a Lieutenant Loeser. Gold fever swept the nation and, despite almost total ignorance of what California was like, many thousands decided to go there.

The safest route was via Cape Horn, but it took 168 days on average from New York and was not a way to prepare the body for life at the diggings. Far more hazardous was the route across Panama, a fever-ridden journey more than 60 years before the building of the canal. Those who did not succumb to disease faced price rackets along the route, and there were similar hazards for those who ventured across Nicaragua. Europeans, including many Britons, rounded the Horn, while Chinese and Hawaiians crossed the Pacific. So did many Australians, among them ex-convicts who were to prove a menace in San Francisco.

The classic route was straight across the Continent, finishing on the California Trail, much of which, as noted in the previous chapter, followed the Oregon Trail. It must be stressed that most of those who crossed this way were far less suited to the rigours of the trail than the earlier pioneers and less prepared for the discipline that was needed. And 1849 was a terrible year for cholera.

One party, starting their journey late in the season, became trapped in that 'seventy-five mile strip of perdition', Death Valley. There were 22 of them, including three women and six children, and finally they camped, two men going on to try and get help. They found it at a mission and returned with horses and food to where the rest lay huddled under wagons.

William Manly, one of the rescuers, fired his gun and a man arose. Manly later described what happened. The gaunt survivor 'threw up his arms high over his head and shouted – "The boys have come! The boys have come." . . . Bennett and Arcane caught us in their arms and embraced us with all their strength, and Mrs Bennett when she came, fell down on her knees and clung to me like a maniac, in the great emotion that came to her, and not a word was spoken.'

Normally, it took three months plus to reach the gold fields. The Manly party took over a year. But at least they remained loyal to each other. Not every group did so.

A hazard of the Cape Horn route was the number of unsuitable ships in use, some being positively unseaworthy. It was too easy for an unscrupulous shipping agent to make a profit. One ship had particularly bad food – 'two bugs for every bean'. And going round the Horn in winter was a grim ordeal. Yet boredom seems to have been the most regular hazard.

Some travellers had fine sentiments wished them. The President of Harvard told the 'Argonauts' travelling aboard the *Edward Everett*, named in his honour: 'Take your Bible in one hand and your New England civilization in the other and make your mark on that country.' Alas, when the 150 members of the expedition, all of them superbly equipped, all unfit from the voyage, and none prepared for the heat of summer, reached the diggings, they did not find them to their liking and gave up within two days.

The best short cut to California was the Panama route, 6,000 using it in 1849 and a record 24,000 hardy travellers using it in 1852. Hazards of the trip included yellow fever, cholera, ticket sharks, wild animals and rides in canoes called bongos. Mules were used in some parts of the 70-mile trip and some rode part of the way as

bundles on the backs of Indians. After these excitements there was chaos at Panama City waiting to acquire a place on a ship; ships' captains had problems because of mass desertions once San Francisco was reached. In 1855, Panama was spanned by rail, by which time there were enough ships to cope with would-be miners.

The Forty-Niners who had come overland mostly headed for Sutter's Fort, as his headquarters was called. It was there that the town of Sacramento was born in November 1848, and became a boom town of 12,000 people a year later. Though there were a number of marvellous finds from the start – one miner found $16,000 worth of gold along one river in only eight working days, while three men found $5,000 under a tree – most Forty-Niners averaged about $100 a month in 1849 itself and far less later. That

may seem a decent return for hard work, but it was not so because a miner's basic cost of living was greatly inflated. Food could be expensive – a restaurant was liable to charge up to $5 for an egg. In reality it was the merchants who grew rich. Domenico Ghirardelli, later a millionaire, started out by selling sweets and chocolates to miners, while the famous Californian millionaires – men like Collis Huntington, the de Youngs and Leland Stanford – could afford to laugh at rivals who called them 'grocers'.

There were some 85,000 Forty-Niners in California, a quarter of whom were not American citizens. Americans – in an area which had only just become theirs – were not keen on outsiders finding gold. Britons and Australians – murderous ex-convicts apart – were welcome enough, and

Above: James Marshall at Sutter's Mill, where he made the strike that triggered off the greatest gold rush of all.

Left: A forest of masts in San Francisco harbour in 1851. Three years earlier the population had been a mere 800.

other Europeans were not unwelcome, but Mexicans had a difficult time and the Chinese fared even worse. Removal of a pigtail to make a good Californian out of a Chinaman was one of the milder torments dispensed, while the fact that Mexicans and South Americans were better at finding gold than the average Forty-Niner did not make for popularity. Lynchings were not infrequent and many Mexicans were driven to crime.

The worst fate was reserved for California's Indians, most of whom were simple, peaceful people with none of the fighting ability of the warriors of the Plains. The catalogue of massacres, gang rapes, kidnapping of thousands of children into slavery and prostitition led to William Brandon's masterly understatement in *The American Heritage Book of Indians* — 'It was not good to be a California Indian in the 1850s.'

The mining camps of the Mother Lode country were usually called towns and each boasted a store of sorts at its heart. In fact, the store was far more than that, being hotel and social centre of the town as well. With less than 8 percent of Californians being female in 1850, all-male dances were only too usual, and lonely miners would gaze in awe at any woman, however homely. One saloon keeper had a fine-looking German girl to sell drinks at 50 cents a glass, but many paid their money just to see her.

Prostitutes started arriving, but many lonely miners wanted wives. Not until the Panama railroad opened in 1855 did the overwhelming shortage of women end, though some Easterners had tried to ease the problem earlier — often without success. One Miss Pellet was going to find 5,000 'virtuous New England women' to head West, but gave up. Slightly

Left: Hermann Herzog's Indian hogans in the Californian Sierras. *For the Indians the Gold Rush was a catastrophe. Few Californian Indians were warriors, most were slain. It was near genocide.*

Below: Californian Gold Rush scenes.

more successful was a Mrs. Farnham, who aimed to supply more than 100 clergyman-vouched ladies. Alas, she embarked with a mere three and got on so badly with the captain that she was put ashore in Chile.

Show business blossomed in California, and not just in San Francisco and Sacramento, with every variety of entertainer touring the mining areas. Actors were liable to be given a rough time if not up to standard, but actresses, even those totally lacking in talent, were sure of a welcome.

Less welcome was the steady growth of lawlessness in the diggings after that first magical season. There

THE DISCOVERY.

"WHISKY GOES"

FREIGHT FOR THE DIGGINGS.

JUMPIN CLAIMS, IS YER?

THE MILL.

MAIN STREET.

THE PACK-MULES.

"JOHN"

SUNDAY AMUSEMENTS.

were no jails on the gold-fields except in camps that were on their way to becoming towns. Elsewhere, those guilty or assumed guilty suffered the lash, banishment from the diggings, or death – which normally meant a lynching. Indians fared worst. Whites could usually get away with raping an Indian girl, whereas, the chief's son who made an indecent gesture at a white girl in 1852 was promptly strung up.

Strict regulations on the fields helped to reduce claim-jumping and other crimes while ordinary robbery often provoked an instant 'neck-tie party'. State historian Andrew Rolle believes that the amount of claim-jumping has been exaggerated, as has the lawlessness of life in the diggings. However in San Francisco crime boomed, along with the population – from 800 in March 1848 to 50,000 in 1855. How the criminals were tamed

the hard way is related in Chapter 10.

There were plenty of San Franciscans ready to help a miner who had struck it rich to enjoy himself, and even moderate gains could ensure a fine night out after a bath and a new suit of clothes. Unfortunately, most of the many brothels included an extra service – picking customers' pockets after they had spent a great deal on drink and more on women. One establishment was nicknamed Murderer's

Corner. Just a few miners came back seeking revenge after being fleeced. One such, Frank Lines, robbed at Madame Reiter's Bagnio, returned to shoot the hostess.

The Big Bonanza

California's was the greatest of all gold rushes, though not in terms of money acquired. The Forty-Niners and those that followed them triggered off the rocket-like rise of the Golden State of California. They also set off America's rise to pre-eminent world power. Because of the Forty-Niners, Western emigration boomed while the completion of the transcontinental railroad in 1869 and resulting flood of immigrants continued the boom. Gold fever made few individuals really rich, but brought mammoth prosperity to the nation.

Meanwhile, miners had the choice of settling down in California, going home, or heading hopefully for new diggings – in America, British Columbia or Australia. Oregon had a notable, though short, gold rush in the 1850s, stained by some particularly cruel atrocities against local Indians. In 1858, many of the miners headed north to British Columbia. There, James Douglas, Governor of Vancouver Island and Chief Factor of the

Hudson's Bay Company, startled the wilder elements among the miners by demanding good behaviour and backing his demands with troops and sailors. The ruffians were kept well in hand.

Far to the south in Nevada, fabulous finds were being made. The place was Virginia City, home of the Big Bonanza, the world-famous Comstock Lode. Its remarkable, high yield veins of silver and gold spawned Bonanza Kings like J.P. Jones. Of him it was said that he counted his dollars by the millions, and had about five times as many millions as he had fingers and toes.

Though gold had been found in 1849 in the area and silver in 1853, part of the Comstock was found in 1859. It was named for Henry Comstock, a good-natured, accident-prone liar and claim jumper who was bought out before anyone realized just how rich the lode was. He committed suicide in 1870, three years before the Big Bonanza made Virginia City world famous.

Even before this sensation $100 million of silver and gold had come from these west Nevada mines between 1859 and 1869. In 1867, the Comstock produced $16½ million. Yet by 1872, it appeared to be virtually exhausted. Then in 1873 came the

Above: A determined-looking quartet of Californians in the 1870s.

Right: Booming Virginia City, Nevada, in the 1860s.

81

greatest of all silver strikes, 1,167 feet down. By using the most modern equipment, 1875 produced $38 million of silver, while all told, the Comstock produced $300 million between 1859–80 in silver and gold. In San Francisco, where these treasures headed, millionaires proliferated.

A notable feature of the Comstock finds was that the richest men were not 'grocers' but hard-working miners, who had begun their rise to fame with picks and shovels. The four leading figures of this drama were John Mackay, Jack O'Brien, James Fair and James Flood, all of them Irish and all merely princes before becoming kings in 1873. Mackay was their emperor. He had arrived penniless in 1859 with O'Brien, who had thrown away their last half dollar for luck as they approached Virginia City, saying: 'Let's enter like gentlemen!'

They deserved to prosper. Mackay would be down one of his mines at 6 am each day, and dedication like that, plus flair and the most advanced mining methods, made Virginia City as efficient as it was renowned.

Bonanza Kings had the good sense not to lose their money from their original finds in the usual ways — gambling, lead-poisoning, drink, lack of business skill, lack of luck, women, or permutations of any of these. Mackay turned himself into an engineer and a geologist as he saw his work level descend from four to 1,500 feet. His judgement was such that he could estimate the worth of a sample of ore almost as well as an assayer. His men, and those of the other Kings, worked regular hours, and miners flocked to join his work force. The city itself was lively, though probably not so lively as Mark Twain's description of its early days in *Roughing It*. He and Dan de Quille, his boss on the *Territorial*

Right: Ready to go down in elevator cages at Cripple Creek, Colorado, a vastly rich mining area.

Below: The site of the fabulous Comstock Lode at Virginia City, Nevada, which produced $300 million between 1859-80.

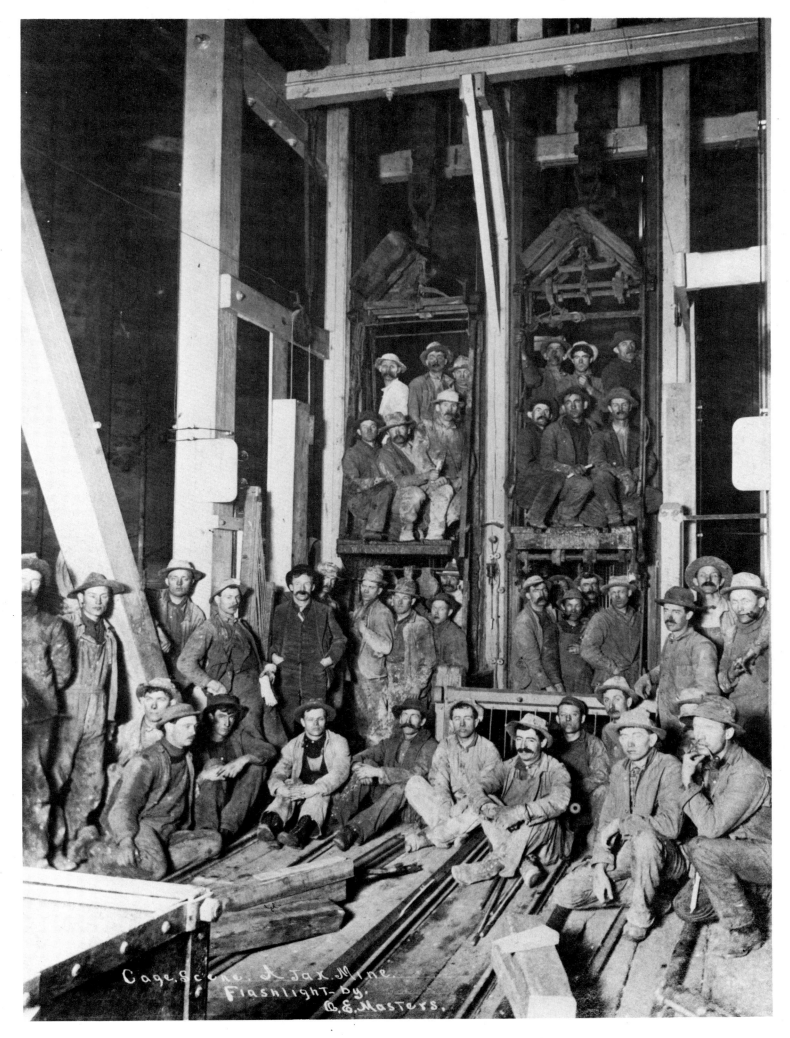

Cage Scene Ajax Mine.
Flashlight by
O. E. Masters.

Opposite page: Discovery of the Last Chance Gulch *by Charles Russell. It happened in Montana in 1864.*

Below: A typically cheery 'Cousin Jack' from Cornwall, whose experience in the Cornish tin mines made him and his fellow Cornishmen much in demand in Colorado.

Enterprise, were quite prepared to lie when space had to be filled. De Quille – his real name was William Wright – wrote the classic book on the Comstock, *The Big Bonanza.*

By 1875, Virginia City's population was 20,000 and respectability had set in. In the good old days, we are told, citizens expected 'a dead man for breakfast every morning'. Today, the city, which never became a complete ghost town, is a great tourist attraction.

Other Bonanzas

Colorado also shot to fame and fortune because of gold and silver, especially silver, as well as copper, lead and zinc. From 1858–1922, gold worth $666,470,261 was produced and silver worth $497,359,655. Early progress was marred because the original rush was deliberately over-promoted by traders along the Missouri in order to end a recession. Agents were hired to actively proclaim a new Eldorado in the West. The result was a fiasco, with 100,000 prospectors heading out in the spring of 1859, few of them miners and few knowing where they were going. Half had returned by the end of the year, though others stayed on to farm.

But the riches were there, as miners found from January 1859 onwards, the first major strike being at Gregory Gulch in May. Finds between 1858–67 were not sensational, but the mining areas were lively spots, and punishments for criminal offences were sometimes more than lively. At Gregory Gulch grand larceny carried a minimum penalty of 15 lashes and a maximum of 300!

It was a rugged life in the mountains, made worse by scurvy from a lack of vegetables and a typhoid-like disease called mountain fever, caused by bad whisky and worse water according to George Willison, author of *Here They Dug Gold.* Central City was the leading town at first, though Denver, junction for three railroads by 1870, was to become the capital, with a population of 135,000 by 1875. The town of Leadville, where Oscar Wilde once lectured to amazed miners, was the nation's silver-mining capital. Though Wilde's subject, *The Ethics of Art,* was a trifle wrong for the occasion, he was elected the 'Prince of good fellows' after first going down a mine then outdrinking his new friends.

A feature of the Colorado mining areas was the presence of Cornish miners, known as Cousin Jacks because all seemed to have such a cousin back home waiting to leave the tin mines and come to America if required. They were skilled, popular and clannish. The best of all Cousin Jack stories concerns 'tributing'. In

some mines, bosses allowed miners to lease a section, the miner paying for it by producing that much more for his company. They could work the section while off duty and this was called 'tributing'.

So popular was tributing that every Cousin Jack (and his wife 'Jennie') was enraged when one particular boss abolished the system. They assembled to talk the matter over and, one of them being a lay preacher, it was suggested that a prayer might be in order.

'Dear Lord,' the preacher enquired, 'does Thee know Simon 'arris, superintendent of the Poor Man Mine? If thee know 'im, we wish for Thee to take 'im and put 'im in 'ell and there let the bugger frizzle and fry until 'e give us back we tributes. And when 'e do,

dear Lord, we ask Thee to take 'im out of 'ell again, and grease 'im up a bit, and turn 'im loose, Amen.'

Though no other bonanzas matched those of California, Nevada and Colorado, many other areas had their period of excitement, notably, Idaho, Montana, the Black Hills of Dakota and, to a lesser degree, New Mexico, Arizona, Utah and Wyoming. The most notorious incidents connected with these will feature in the chapters devoted to Law and Disorder and the Indian Wars. Which leaves us with the last and most rugged Rush of them all.

The Klondike Stampede

A little gold had been found in Alaska and Canada's Yukon Territory before

the famous strike of 1896. There were miners on each side of the ill-defined border from the 1880s, men with experience, not greenhorns, and most of them were Americans. Only the extreme remoteness of the Yukon explains why the Stampede came as late as it did.

The great day was August 17th, the place Rabbit Creek, renamed Bonanza Creek. The finders were the American George Carmack and his two Indian friends, Skookum Joe and Tagish Charley. Their find resulted from a tip given to them by a Canadian, Robert Henderson, who considered the creek a likely area, having found a little gold there himself.

The three men struck it so rich that they understandably did a war dance, described later by Carmack as a combination of Scottish hornpipe, Indian fox trot, syncopated Irish jig, and Siwash hula. They had found gold lying like a giant cheese sandwich between slabs of rock, and when the news broke, other prospectors rushed to the area.

Henderson arrived there late and failed to strike it rich, then or later. Anti-Indian remarks that he directed at Carmack's friends may have ruined his chances, though Canadians regard him as the finder, while Americans support the dancing trio.

At first the outside world knew nothing about the strike. A few Mounties arrived to keep order, setting a pattern that ensured the rule of law in the Klondike, but not until winter was over did the outside world receive the electrifying news. Meanwhile, fortunes were made and sometimes lost in the local boom village of Dawson, where gold soon became less valuable than salt. The trickle that was

to become a flood began as miners across Alaska heard the news, then, in July 1898, two boatloads of Bonanza Kings brought the joyous tidings to Seattle and San Francisco, and the world went mad. The papers dubbed the disease Klondicitis.

Unfortunately, the world hardly knew where the Klondike was, and most of those who feverishly decided to go there were woefully ill-equipped. Some were to find themselves frozen in for the winter along the Yukon, having endured wretched voyages in boats totally unsuited to ocean travel. One of the worst routes there was the Ashcroft Trail through British Columbia, which involved a nightmare journey, while the Edmonton Trail was a killer – literally, for out of 2,000 who set out at least 500 died. It was promoted as a 90-day trip by Edmonton's Board of Trade, yet only 100 or so made it along the 2,500-mile route – after the gold rush was over.

In fact, there was only one realistic – though very rugged – way. This was a sea trip to Alaska, landing at Skagway on American territory, then choosing one of the two terrible passes, the Chilkoot or the White, and, after crossing them into Canadian territory, building boats beside Lake Bennett while waiting for the ice to break for the dangerous journey on the Yukon river to Dawson.

The White was lower than the Chilkoot, but was also a longer route that involved swamps, rivers of mud, and a path which was only two feet wide at one point with a 500-foot (152-metre) drop below. Overloaded horses, some of them unbroken, 'died like mosquitoes in the first frost and from Skagway to Bennett they rotted in heaps'. So wrote Jack London about the scenes that shamed the Stampede.

The Chilkoot was a short cut that involved a four-mile climb to its sum-

Above: The Chilkoot Pass in 1898. The addition of an aerial tramway for baggage (top right) helped the Stampeders, though the going remained rugged.

mit. Much too steep for horses, it was climbed by an endless chain of Stampeders, bent almost double by their loads. Haunting photographs have captured their ordeal so vividly that they have come to embody the spirit of all those who sought for gold. Not until most of the 22,000 who climbed the Chilkoot had traversed it was an aerial tramway with a copper-steel cable erected to carry goods up.

To prevent starvation in and around Dawson, Superintendent Sam Steele of the Mounties ordered that every Stampeder must bring in a year's food supply. The tops of both passes were guarded to ensure that his order was obeyed – an order that forced each stampeder to make journey after journey to the top to get his ton of goods up. An experienced climber found no difficulties, but few were experienced and most were ill and underfed. They

climbed in a line that became known as the Chilkoot Lock-Step, roasting or freezing in their heavy clothes, which stank because they lived in them. Only a few could afford to hire carriers. And just a few romped up the slope – the Indian who reached the summit with a 350-lb (159-kg) barrel on his back and an American who took a 125-lb (57-kg) plough up the final nightmare section – for worst of all were the last 150 feet (46 metres). Climbers had dug out some steps and were liable to charge for their use. As for anyone daring to rest by stepping out of line, he was likely to have to wait a day to get back into it.

Yet men, women and children from many nations pressed upwards, and even included dancing girls, Dawson-bound, an elderly English nobleman with his valet, and a German woman of 70.

Left: A street scene in Dawson.

Once at the top, all were finally out of the clutches of 'Soapy' Smith and his gang. 'Soapy' had flourished as a con man in Colorado, helped by a very respectable appearance. His nickname came from convincing miners there that the five dollar shaving soap sticks he was selling might have dollars under their wrappers. The first stick sold would have a $100 with it, the rest were almost all soap!

'Soapy' reigned in Skagway, main gateway to the Klondike, and he had it in his pocket. The inspiration behind many a Western, he controlled town, law, the routes to the passes and the carriers on them. His hand-picked gang were everywhere, a most notable con man being 'Reverend' Bowers, who warned newcomers of the town's temptations, but leading them, if they really insisted on a little gambling, to men they could 'really' trust. Few bankrolls survived.

Sham enterprises abounded including particularly mean ones, such as the telegraph office where – for a good price – a telegram was allegedly sent to a loved one at home. And if by any chance anyone escaped the many traps, there was always fine-looking Old Man Tripp, allegedly returning from the mines, who dispensed phoney information to those who still had some money after leaving Soapy's Skagway. One of the few to survive the gang's ministrations was Bishop Rowe of Alaska. He had a pouch of gold stolen, but when the thief found out who he was, he gave the pouch back.

'Why do you give this back?' asked the bishop.

'Hell, Bishop!' said the robber, 'I'm a member of your congregation.'

Finally, the townspeople, many of whom actually liked the charming Soapy, had had enough of him, especially as their town's name was beginning to suffer. Fears of losing their key role on the road to Dawson influenced them, as did their finer citizens. One of them, a surveyor named Frank Reid, led a rebellion against Soapy, shooting him dead, though receiving a mortal wound himself. The gang was rounded up, but not lynched. Law and order had arrived at last. Instead, the gang were expelled and 11 of the 26 served prison sentences.

A month earlier – in June, 1898 – the main body of stampeders reached Dawson by river. The ice had cracked on Lake Bennett on May 29th and 7,124 'homemade' craft set out on their 500-mile journey. Some 'boats' were coffins. Miles Canyon was crisis point for these unskilled sailors, a canyon, with a whirlpool followed by rapids. There were some disasters and ten deaths, but Sam Steele, soon to be known as the Lion of the Yukon, suddenly arrived and brought order out of the chaos. He ordered every boat checked and guided through the rapids while the women and children walked below them.

A few had a head start on the rest, including one smart operator who reached Dawson with 2,400 eggs which he sold for $3,600. The main armada appeared on June 8th, and Dawson became an instant booming gold rush centre. Boats arrived from

Above: The all important business of weighing the gold.

Right: The notorious conman and ruler of Skagway, Soapy Smith — bearded, and with his hand on the bar — until the town rose against him.

Opposite page, left to right: Two cradles and what seems to be an unfinished sluice in the Yukon in 1898.

their long, partly ice-bound passage up the Yukon, and Dawson, which had a mere 5,000 population in mid-1897, now had between 25,000 and 40,000. Estimates varied. Most of those who had arrived were too late, the best claims having been staked out. Some were despondent; others needed the merest rumour to race after the phantom gold; still more became virtual sightseers. Yet most seem to have been proud just to have got to the Klondike. They had reached their goal and the memory would remain with them all their lives. Unlike so many seekers after gold, they were true adventurers.

Dawson, thanks to the Mounties, was unique among boom towns. In the fabulous year of 1898 there was not a single murder. And, as in the first magical season of 1848 in California, men could leave their cabin doors unlocked even if there was gold inside.

A year later, companies were buying up claims and the 'poor man's rush' was over, while in 1900 most miners who had stayed on decided to head for a new strike at Nome in Alaska. Between 1897 and 1905, the Klondike produced $100 million, and mining still goes on though Dawson has a mere 500 people. Trains go through the White, while the Chilkoot remains a silent reminder of stirring times. Thanks to the Klondike, America's North-western coastal cities threw off a slump, and Vancouver and Edmonton also benefitted. Many Canadian Stampeders prospered in later life and many were decorated in World War One. After the Klondike, nothing seemed impossible.

And the men who struck it rich in the first place? George Carmack died rich in 1922. Tagish Charley did well too, becoming a successful hotel owner and a splendid host until, after too convivial an evening, he fell off a bridge and drowned. Skookum Jim, though he received $90,000 a year from his mine, never stopped prospecting and died from overtaxing his splendid physique in 1916. For poor Henderson, nothing went right, even the little he made being stolen. Though the Canadians gave him a pension of $200 a month, he never ceased looking for his bonanza until his death in 1933.

Right: Snake Hips Lulu, one of the attractions of gold rush Dawson, where law and order reigned, along with fun.

Below: Front Street in Nome, Alaska in 1899. There was a rush to the area after the Klondike Stampede.

CHAPTER NINE
COWBOY

Unlike other Frontier immortals such as Custer, Geronimo and Hickok, the American cowboy remains anonymous. Glamour surrounds the memory of this hired hand on horseback, but it was not always so. A century ago most people used 'cowboy' as another term for desperado. It is to Buffalo Bill Cody that the credit belongs for cleaning up their shoddy image and beginning the myth that still survives.

His instrument was a 6ft 5in (1.96 m) cowpuncher named William Levi Taylor, whom he transformed into 'Buck' Taylor, 'The King of the Cowboys'. Audiences were assured that Buck was 'as amiable as a child' and, equipped with this knowledge, could enjoy his taming of a bucking bronco without siding with the wrong animal.

That was in 1884, and the word 'cowboy' still looms so large in the minds of millions that many call all Westerns 'cowboy' films despite the fact that only a few are about that mythical breed.

There was a flourishing cattle industry in the West long before the Declaration of Independence. A French trader saw 'thousands of cows, bulls, horses and mares' in Texas in 1715. Ranches grew steadily larger, one at Goliad having 40,000 head. California, too, was cattle country. When Stephen Austin led his American party into Texas in 1821, cattle were brought as well with permission. By 1830, there were 100,000 or so, and a fifth of them American. The breeds amalgamated, then, during the Texas revolution, ran wild.

Naturally, there were many raids north after the revolution by Mexicans who had lost their herds, but the Texas cattle industry began to grow, the newcomers learning from the Mexicans even though they despised them.

The word 'cowboy' had travelled far by this time. Originally it meant exactly that on both sides of the Atlantic where boys tended cows, but by the 1760s it was being used by the Dutch patroons of New York colony to describe rebellious tenants. In the Revolution, Loyalist guerillas who stole Patriot (or anybody else's) cows were called cowboys, and the word headed westwards with the first American pioneers.

Cowboy, cow herder and cow driver were all terms used in early Texas, but not yet cowpuncher, bosses being called cattlemen, as well as ranchers and stockmen. Grandest of all were the later cattle barons/cattle kings. By the time the Civil War broke out in 1861, the cattle business, too often thought of as a post-war phenomenon, was starting to boom, with trails to Missouri, Louisiana and, especially, California. One herd actually reached New York.

The war saw the collapse of the industry, but before relating how it recovered, the two principal characters of the story, the cowboy and

the Longhorn must be properly introduced.

Longhorns were long-legged, lanky-bodied, mean, moody and, in their way, magnificent. Fast moving, with horns that could measure up to seven feet tip to tip, generations of freedom had made wild animals of them. A man on foot confronted with a number of Longhorns felt more than somewhat uneasy – with good reason, as Colonel Richard Dodge described

Above: The Texas Longhorn, which, along with the Texas cowboy, made history. Happily, neither is extinct.

Opposite page: Roping a Steer: *By Charles Russell.*

Below: Texas cowboys relaxing in town.

Below: Frederic Remington's Arizona Cowboy.

in *The Hunting Grounds of the Great West*. During a march in the war against Mexico of 1846–48, a soldier fired at a wild bull:

The bull immediately charged; and the soldier, taking to his heels, ran into the column. The bull, undaunted by the number of his enemies, charged headlong, scattering several regiments like chaff. He finally escaped unhurt, having demoralized and put to flight an army which, a few days later, covered itself with glory by victoriously encountering five times its number of human enemies.

Longhorns prospered on their diet of buffalo grass and grama, a grass which survives droughts and could be enjoyed through the winters. The beasts were hard to find in the spring, hiding in thick brush, but were driven from cover by mosquitos in the summer, which helped in rounding them up.

The Texas cowboy engaged in the

94

roundup was mainly a first or second generation Texan of Southern ancestry. He was paid a mere $30 a month, and though he craved excitement, much of his life was monotonous and lonely. After the Civil War, he was a bitter man, and the natural enemy of Northern lawmen in charge of cowtowns at the end of the trail.

The cowboy worked hard and was almost always loyal to his friends and his boss. He looked after his horses better than Mexicans and Indians did, liked practical jokes, revered good women, and was liable to tell anyone talkative: 'Save part of your breath for breathing.'

His weapon was the six-shooter, though he could rarely match a full-time gunfighter's skill. Most cowboys hated Indians, despised Mexicans and, though they would work with Blacks, refused to socialize with them. They had little time for townspeople and their politest word for settlers was sodbusters, who were also known as nesters, squatters, wool-hat people and clodbusters. Even worse were sheepmen and their 'woolies' who allegedly ruined a range and fouled waterholes. Mutton never touched a cowboy's lips (allegedly), and many sheepherders and thousands of sheep

were slaughtered before cattle and sheep were finally allowed to co-exist. As late as 1909, there was a savage attack on sheepmen in Wyoming.

On the Ranch

The cowboy waking on the prairie was likely to begin the day by putting on his hat, probably a stetson, an all purpose hat that sheltered him against the elements and was suitable for drinking purposes, human or equine. The bandanna round his neck could prevent sunburn, mop up sweat and keep dust out of his nose and mouth. He wore a collarless flannel or cotton shirt and long johns in ordinary weather, while his tight woollen pants were worn without a belt or suspenders (braces), both being uncomfortable when working. Tobacco was carried in his vest (waistcoat) pocket, and so could be used when riding.

His boots and spurs were of Spanish origin, though the latter were less cruel than a *vaquero's*. Chaps, pronounced 'shaps', were vital leg protectors especially in brush country, some being close-fitting 'shotgun' chaps, the others wide 'batwing' ones. On the northern ranges woolly ones were used.

Mexicans used a 60-foot (18-m) long *reata* (rope), but Texans used lariats of from 25–35 feet (7.6–10 m), while their saddles were adapted from Spanish ones, the lariat being secured to the horn. A hand's six-gun spent most of its time in his bedroll except when on the trail. The Winchester '73 was the favourite rifle from the mid-Seventies, but on the range there was little gunfire, whatever movies suggest. What there was plenty of was hard work looking after dumb critters on a sea of grass.

Trail herding was the high spot of the year, but the spring and fall roundups were also major events. The spring roundup in the early days was for branding new calves and gathering cows of four or more years for the drive northwards. Later, when the trail drives were over, it was simply for branding calves. The fall round up was for branding new arrivals and ones missed earlier, and, in later times, for collecting beeves for shipment to market.

Mustanging – hunting wild horses – made for lively action, though not at the gallop, which would have ruined good horses.

Winter was a dull period and some hands were paid off, others being kept

on without pay but with their board free. A laid off cowboy could be sure of a meal at any ranch he visited out of season, such was the law of range hospitality. Many hands hit town, having been forbidden alcohol on the ranch. Some ranchers forbade gambling as well. Their fun included shooting off the end of someone's cigar in the bar, for 'parking' firearms was mainly confined to wild cowtowns where tough lawmen had to control cowboys roaring for lively action after months on the trail. Good women were universally respected; meanwhile, there were 'soiled doves' in town to provide some comfort.

The best paid job out of season was that of wolfer – killing wolves. The best method was to haunt a wolf's lair when it was slowed down by food. Then one crawled into the lair holding a candle and a six gun. As the explosion often blew the candle out, the job was not for the nervous.

In the summer a cowboy's day began at 4 am. He had almost certainly slept in the open rather than in the vermin-ridden bunkhouse that smelled of dung, tobacco, boots and

sweat. The hand crawled out of his 'tarp', a tarpaulin with flaps, and which could be packed with blankets and contained his war-bag, a possession that included six-gun and ammunition, and his razor. 'Cookie' would be yelling for hands to 'Come and git it' and come they did, Cookie being an essential person. There was little chance of a wash, but there were tricks to be learnt, like dry-cleaning your clothes over an ant-hill, Jim Bridger style.

As soon as possible, a cowboy was mounted, which was the way he liked to work. He had eight to a dozen horses to use and would select one from the remuda, which was looked after by a young wrangler, a humble job, but important and a fine way to get started. The small saddle horses the hand used were his friends, skilled, like himself, in the ways of cows. Jobs to be done included getting Longhorns out of bogs – a two-man operation, with vicious horns livening things up – and putting out prairie fires. Less active ones included applying carbolic acid and axle grease to sores on cattle made by the eggs of

blowflies that later turned into screwworms.

The worst job was riding line, which became riding fence when barbed wire was invented. There were line camps at the extremities of a ranch where one of two men had to stay in summer or – worse – in winter, patrolling, seeing that the ranch's cattle did not stray, or interlopers get in, likewise rustlers and wild animals. The hand or hands endured a dugout home, riding fence being the worse job because more monotonous. Some men went crazy, one such being found by his friends in the spring shooting at his coat and hat which decorated a tree stump. 'I'm gonna get the son of a bitch before he gets me,' he was shouting.

Round-ups were simple affairs after barbed wire was introduced in the 1870s, but could spread over enormous areas earlier, with stockmen all helping each other in these bi-annual assemblies. Skilled 'reps' had to know all the local brands, and the whole affair was master-minded by an elected leader. Each outfit helped pay for the operation, while each area was combed until every stockman had collected his stock – from timber, draws and the brush. The cattle were driven into the centre of a circle, reps looking them over to spot their own stock. At the circle's centre, the animals were 'cut' – segregated – then branding and castrating was done. Two cowboys worked together at cutting out, mounted on good cutting horses, but even then it needed great skill to prevent the 'beef' from regaining the herd.

Skilled men were in little danger at roundups except when roping. As well as heavy falls, a finger or thumb could be lost after a cowboy had hitched his rope around his saddle horn and an angry steer had pulled it taut.

It gradually became standard prac-

tice to dehorn Longhorns with outsize horns before they went up the trail because of the injuries they could inflict on each other. And the trail had many far more dangerous hazards.

Enter a Saviour

Longhorn meat did not appeal to sophisticated palates, but the thousands who had headed West before the Civil War were glad to eat it, and so were the hordes of European emigrants who later poured into the U.S.A.

Yet the cattle industry had its problems. It was not just the Civil War that ruined it for a time, with thousands of Longhorns running wild and ranches running down as owners and hands joined the Confederate ranks. The

Longhorns carried a disease called variously, Texas, Mexican or Spanish fever. Though the Longhorns themselves were immune from it, the ticks that the cattle carried played havoc with Northern cattle. Quarantine laws were passed and some Kansas counties banned southern cattle. During the war thousands of cattle were killed by drought and when peace came the industry seemed ruined.

In fact, the time was ripe for a beef bonanza. The North needed meat, so did the railroad workers, and in the spring of 1866, things looked bright.

It was to be a troubled year, however. Those who went up the trail not only had to pay money to the Five Civilized Tribes of Indian Territory, which was reasonable enough, but found themselves atacked by outlaw bands, many of them ex-guerrillas. Some made tick fever the excuse for their savagery. Fortunately, 1867 was to be very different.

The year began badly enough, but a saviour named Joseph McCoy appeared, a 29-year-old cattle dealer who understood the whole livestock market. He decided that Chicago should become the headquarters of the beef industry and that the nation should give its allegiance to beef rather than pork. St. Louis was currently the headquarters of the trade.

A shipping point was the key to success, and in mid-1867 he chose a tiny point on the railroad called Abi-

lene, which had a dozen or so cabins and a prairie dog colony in the main and only street. Trains could stop there and there was a hook for mail. The hamlet was officially in the zone banned to Texas cattle, but it was so short of settlers that the ban was not enforced in the area.

By September 1st, he had a shipping yard for 1,000 cattle, a barn and an office, and was supervising construction of his three-storey Drover's Cottage, soon to be famous. He made a friend of the Governor of Kansas and sent word to Texan drovers looking for a market. (In the early days drovers contracted with ranchers to take cattle up the trail, selling them at trail's end. Later, ranchers sent stock led by trail bosses, though some took their own herds north.)

There was a modest but encouraging start to the trade in 1867, the first shipment from Abilene being on September 5th, with 20 cars bound for Chicago. In all, 35,000 were despatched. The trail from Texas was the immortal Chisholm Trail, named for a Scots-Indian trader who had blazed it. It ended at Wichita, but the cattle went on to Abilene. The first boom year was 1868 when 75,000 reached the blossoming cowtown. Forty-five thousand were sent East by rail, the rest being driven north to found new ranges in Wyoming and Montana. The greatest year of all for Abilene was 1871 when there were 600,000 cattle in south-central Kansas. This was too many for Abilene to handle, which helped the rise of Newton.

Meanwhile, back in 1866, Charlie Goodnight and Oliver Loving had blazed the trail that bore their name to New Mexico, being followed later by the legendary John Chisum. Loving headed north to Colorado. These trails were tougher and more dangerous than the Chisholm, as was that led by Nelson Story to the goldfields of Montana in 1866. He went up the Bozeman Trail when it had already been denuded of whites by Red Cloud's War (see Chapter 13). The party got through mainly because his 27 men had Remington breech-loaders at a time when most Indians were still using bows. They were also very determined.

Up the Trail

Between 1,000 and 2,000 Longhorns made up the average trail herd, some six to 12 cowboys being in charge of them. As on the ranch, pay was $30 a week, with $40 for top hands, and a month's wages at the end of the trail for the journey home.

A drover contracted with ranchers then chose his cowboys, plus a wrangler for the horses. He bought a chuck wagon and hired the all-important cook. Each Longhorn had a special, extra brand for the trail. Later, when a rancher hired a trail boss, he would meet the herd in the north, having gone on ahead by boat or rail. Herds usually started in March and April, though the size of Texas affected starting times. Good pasture was more easily found early, and the Longhorns often grazed on northern grass to be 'beefed up' after the trail and so made more attractive to buyers.

Some herds were all steers, others mixed, and most were four- or five-year olds. Ten to 12 miles a day was the average pace. At Forth Worth, Texas, food was bought for a month or more, for in early days there were no stores from there until Kansas was reached. The basic foodstuffs were bacon, flour and coffee.

The best trail hands were made pointers, the leaders of the herd. Swing men rode beside it, then flank men, then the unfortunate drag men or tail riders who 'ate dust' and looked after the weaklings, the slow critters and the dumb ones. Fortunately, drag work was done in rotation. Some Longhorns were leaders by nature, the most famous being Charley Goodnight's Old Blue, who was considered worth a dozen hands by his master. A snob, Old Blue refused to mix with the herd and expected to be fed by the cook. This not-so-dumb Longhorn went up the trail time and again.

The boss rode ahead scouting for water and pasture. At 11 am the men had their first meal since an early breakfast, and camp was made before dusk.

The herd was put in a circle and the hands had their main meal. The cattle gradually settled and the cook set his wagon's tongue with the North Star, the herd's compass. At intervals of two hours or so the two-man night guard was changed. If the herd was restless, they hummed or sang – even in a storm, for the herd had to hear a human voice. About midnight, the herd got to its feet for a stretch and then settled itself again. Cowboys only took off their boots and belt if the

Above: Cattle Drive from Texas.
Herds were between 1,000 and 2,000
longhorns.

Left: Indian cowboys – either Caddo or
Kickapoo. Warriors preferred it to
farming.

weather was very hot, and either had
their night horse picketed nearby or
slept with reins in their hands. In a big
outfit, the wrangler might be relieved
by a nighthawk. He also had to help
Cookie with dishwashing and wood
for the fire.

Trouble amongst the men was rare
on the trail. There was too much else
to worry about – rustlers, Indians,
enraged settlers, swollen rivers,
floods, prairie fires, stampedes. No
wonder the exhausted men went wild
in the cowtowns. Apart from the boss
and the cook, very few were aged
more than 30.

The two most dangerous regular
dangers of the trail were stampedes
and river crossings. In the spring and
fall, there were liable to be floods
resulting in the deaths of horses and
cattle and sometimes cowboys.

Quicksands were another hazard.

The boss chose the spot for crossing
and tried to avoid the sun shining in
the cattle's faces. Supervised by the
men, the cattle crossed in groups of 30
or so or en masse, and sometimes
everything went perfectly. But an
unexpected sound, an eddy, a floating
log could cause chaos, the herd cir-
cling wildly in mid-stream. The cowboys were forced to ride into the
melée, risking life and limb to try and
get their charges to the bank. Yet the
dangers of rivers crossing, the occasional deaths, were as nothing compared with the nightmare of a
stampede.

This chaotic rush usually started at
night, occasionally triggered by a
single, frightened Longhorn, and the
most likely times were in rainy seasons
or during storms. A thunderclap

could start one, so could the striking of a match. Electric storms found the hands extra tense, but at least they were ready, with the cows, horns glowing with phosphorescent light.

When the stampede started every hand not already mounted leapt on his horse and raced with the rest after the herd. They had to get them in a circle, gradually narrowing it, though not too much or those in the centre would be hurt. Inevitably, there were deaths followed by funerals on the 'lone prairie'.

As soon as one stampede was contained another could start. Some ended after 5 miles, others took a week and covered hundreds of miles. The worst recorded loss was 2,700 Longhorns who crashed into a Texas ravine in 1876. Rustlers and Indians sometimes caused stampedes. Some happened for no apparent cause at all. There were amazing escapes, including one man who was thrown by his falling horse on top of the racing cattle and carried some distance on the moving platform. When he rolled off to safety, he had merely a few bruises.

What happened when the cowboys hit town is related in the next chapter. Each of the cowtowns had a period of

gaudy glory, then settled down to a less lively existence. Many, like Abilene, Dodge City, Wichita, have achieved legendary status.

During the early 1880s, there were fewer and fewer long drives from Texas, and other ranges, especially in Montana, Colorado, Wyoming, flourished. Part of the Chisholm was now farmland, and new cattle towns like Cheyenne, Ogalalla, Miles City and Julesburg were flourishing.

Above: Charles Russell's Cattle Drive. *The artist had been a cowboy and had lived with Indians.*

Opposite page: Frederic Remington's vivid picture of a stampede. Some stampedes went on for days.

Below: Remington's Riding the Line of the Wire Fence.

Changes on the Range

On November 24th, 1874, J.F. Glidden took out the first patent for barbed wire. There was hostility at first, but when it was realized that the cattle would avoid the wire just as they avoided thorns, the new system conquered the ranges. By 1883, the company using Glidden's patent was producing 600 miles of wire a day. The wire provoked some gunsmoke as every moviegoer knows, but like the hostility between cattlemen and sheepmen, it has been exaggerated. On a more domestic level postmen suffered, travelling many miles round the wire to deliver mail. A Colorado company wired over a million acres.

Huge amounts of American as well as British money were invested in the Western cattle business, but more significant was the import of British stock. Better meat was needed, so purebred and high grade bulls, especially Herefords, crossed the ocean and reached the West. These were best able to survive the most rugged conditions and became the favourite of Western ranchers.

But even these could not be sure of surviving the nightmare winter of 1886–87. Some ranchers lost all their stock and cowboy Teddy Blue's estimate that by March 15th, 1887, 60 percent of all Montana's cattle were dead seems not exaggerated. He called it hell without the heat. At least an old-timer had told him how to dress for the occasion, warning him that he must be warm enough to lie on the prairie if he should break a leg. So the English-born Teddy put on two pairs of wool socks, another pair that came up to his knees, with moccasins over them and overshoes over the moccasins. He wore two suits of heavy underwear, pants, overalls, chaps, plus a heavy shirt, and he made sleeves from a woman's stockings. He also wore mittens and gloves, a blanket-lined coat and a sealskin cap. In his book *We Pointed Them North* he says he was warm enough, 'but not any too warm'.

Cattle Kings

This appalling disaster at least had the effect of making the cattle industry more professional, if less glamorous. Cattle Kings remained larger than life

Right: Two cowboys of the Hashknife outfit.

Below: Mr. and Mrs. J Selman keeping an eye on their property. Note the chuck wagon. Ranchers rarely wore guns – their cowboys were known to be excellent guardians of the boss.

104

figures, men like Richard King whose empire in southern Texas exists to this day, like Granville Stuart, who, having made Montana's first gold strike, became its greatest cattleman. Rustlers had every reason to hate him and his Vigilantes, but cowboys liked working for him, for he paid well, helped them in trouble and let them own their own cattle. His friends disapproved, fearing that it would lead to branding mavericks and to outright rustling, but he believed that men with a stake in the range would be much less likely to steal.

Some would-be cattle kings failed spectacularly, like the French Marquis de Morés; some ranches were of fantastic size, like the XIT which had 3 million acres in Texas and, later, a huge spread in Montana. General Manager Boyce ordered his men one day in 1890: 'Keep your eye on the North Star, and drive straight ahead until you can wet your feet in the waters of the Yellowstone.'

Cattlemen were seen at their most arrogant in the Johnson County War, dealt with in the next chapter. The last great trailing year was 1884 when 300,000 cattle went up the trails.

Every year after that the numbers fell dramatically until in the 1890s there were no drives. The open range and the old days were dead, but ten million cattle had been driven north from Texas, the greatest migration of domestic animals in history. Texas had prospered mightily from them and so had Kansas, whatever its citizens felt about the men and boys who drove the herds. Beef had indeed replaced pork as the national meat, and the meat of cattle descended from Herefords, Shorthorns and the rest not only satisfied the national appetite and ended the era of the Longhorns, but turned them into museum pieces – as pets or for Western movies.

Cowboys – the hired hands on horseback, or, as their detractors have sneered, social misfits – discovered that mutton was eatable and that sodbusters were quite tolerable, and vice versa. The glamour remains, colouring attitudes to today's cowboys.

The good old days died hard and, indeed, in the mid-1880s one small spot in Kansas tried to resurrect them. At the time there was talk of a national trail right up to the Canadian border, talk that stemmed from Texas, as

A stylishly dressed Wyoming cowboy.

Remington's The Fall of the Cowboy. *The open range has been fenced with barbed wire and the cowboy forced to get off his horse.*

Longhorns were no longer wanted in the North. The spot where it was all going to happen was Trail City, which straddled the Colorado–Kansas line.

Trail City had only been founded in 1885 and its demise came in 1887, though Colorado was still a 'wet' state, Kansas having become a dry one. It died when the national trail idea died, but it is recalled for two stories.

The first was that as it was split by the state line, a wanted man could elude a sheriff with little effort in either direction. The second relates how the sporting gals of Trail City used to ride over to Coolidge, Kansas, two miles eastwards, advertising their attractions in a highly effective manner. They were all stark naked.

Just over 20 years earlier, when Texas was still trying to recover from the destruction of the cattle industry, the *Galveston News* of August 16th,

1866 was noting a phenomenon among young Texans. It would be 18 years before Buffalo Bill Cody would publicly transform the image of the cowboy that existed in most minds. In Texas it never had needed changing. The reporter on the *News* wrote:

There is not a boy of American parentage learning a trade or reading for a profession west of the Colorado. Our youths have souls above the mechanical arts. The little children, as early as they can walk, pilfer their mother's tape and make lassos to rope the kittens and the ducks. The boys, as soon as they can climb on a pony, are off to the prairie to drive stock. As they advance toward manhood, their highest ambition is to conquer a pitching mustang or throw a wild beef by the tail.

CHAPTER TEN
LAW AND DISORDER

It was a common expression in the cowtown of Newton that they had a man every morning for breakfast. Sensible lawmen, some of whom survived into old age, knew the facts of Frontier life. Wild Bill Hickok, murdered in 1876, said in 1871: 'If you have to shoot a man, shoot him in the guts near the navel. You may not make a fatal shot, but he will get a shock that will paralyse his brain and arm so much that the fight is all over.' Such frankness is a far cry from Hollywood style shoot-outs at high noon fought under a mythical Code of the West.

The real, unwritten code was roughly this: kill an unarmed man and it ranks as murder, but if your opponent was armed – even if he was standing with his back to you or was sound asleep, the chances are that you will get off by pleading self defence at your trial. However, your victim's

friends may string you up or shoot you.

Though earlier 'Wests' were often even wilder, the Wild West that gave rise to the West of legend that was to conquer the world's imagination was basically the period from the end of the Civil War in 1865 to around 1900. This West, as opposed to Hollywood's version, was devoid of glamour, some of the scenery apart. It was a combination of squalor and bravery, violence and boredom, high adventure and gunsmoke and sudden death.

The 'stars' of this most famous West were the gunfighters. Films have portrayed them as supermen or dastardly villains or sometimes, recently, as homicidal maniacs. In fact, they were only too human beings who stood out from the rest in dangerous times because they were ready to kill if necessary and knew how to.

A far cry from the lone lawman was Vigilante law, understandable in areas where there was no law at all, but looked at askance by many today because of known cases of innocent men being 'jerked to Jesus' and of executing those who, for one reason or other, were in the way.

Gold Rush San Francisco had outbreaks of Vigilante fever, 1851 being a classic year. In February a well-known storekeeper named Jansen was beaten up and robbed in his store and the alleged culprits were caught and tried. During the trial a mob of several thousand invaded the court and tried to hang the alleged villains, desisting when it was decided to hold a special court. This failed to

Overleaf: Dispute Over a Deal *by Frederic Remington.*

Below: A gang of Kansas 'Free-staters' who rescued a man named Doy (seated) from jail in 1859. Note the impressive display of weapons.

agree and the men were tried again and convicted. Just in time the real culprits were found.

Very different was the first Committee of Vigilance of San Francisco, founded the same year to deal with genuine ruffians who had turned the city into a nightmare jungle after dark. The culprits were known as the Sydney Ducks, an unsavoury gang of Australian ex-convicts and ticket-of-leave men who specialized in murder and arson, the latter followed by looting. A large-scale fire provoked enraged citizens to kill some of the Ducks, but as 2,000 buildings had been destroyed something more was needed. The Committee that was formed consisted of some 200 citizens pledged 'to watch, pursue, and bring to justice the outlaws infesting the city, through the regularly constituted courts, if possible, through more summary courts, if necessary . . . no thief, burglar, incendiary, or assassin, shall escape punishment, either by quibbles of the law, the insecurity of prisons, the carelessness or corruption of the police, or a laxity of those who pretend to administer justice.'

One John Jenkins, a former Australian convict, chose this moment to steal a strongbox. Bells rang out to assemble the Committee and the next morning, despite efforts by his friends to rescue him, he was hanged. Then 183 vigilantes signed a public statement to the effect that all of them were equally responsible. Over the next three months three more criminals were hanged, one was whipped, 14 deported, one banished, 41 discharged and 15 handed over to the authorities. Then, early in 1853, having done their jobs, the vigilantes stood down, having enjoyed almost universal support in the city.

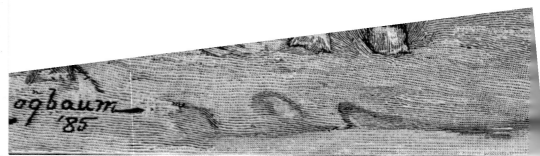

Right: The Vigilantes *by Rufus R. Zogbaum (1885). Vigilantes kept order where there was no law, but were liable to make mistakes.*

In 1856, two murders, complete with the stench of corruption, led to a new vigilance committee, hangings, banishments and – again – the committee standing down. Because of the vigilantes, the city enjoyed some years of reasonably good government, and the fact that these vigilantes were prepared to stand down as soon as possible hardly suggests they were bully boys. Yet the other side of the coin was witnessed by Edward Buffum in the gold-fields. Five men were given 39 lashes apiece after being caught robbing a gambler, then three of them were accused of murder and an attempted armed robbery months earlier. They were sentenced to die by 200 'jurors', even though they were unable to plead, one being Chilean and two French. Buffum was nearly hanged himself for daring to stand up for them.

Better vigilante justice was handed out by vigilantes in Montana, who in 1864 rid the area of a Napoleon of crime named Henry Plummer. He looked every inch a man to be trusted, a paragon of integrity, despite a record of robbery and violence elsewhere. His masterstroke was to get himself made sheriff of Bannack, Montana, in the heart of the gold-mining area. This made it so much simpler to organize and run his 100-strong army of road agents – highwaymen. He ran a string of lodging houses near the mines and packed them with his own men. Every stagecoach that the 'staff' considered worth robbing was marked, and his boys, known as 'The Innocents' sported special knots in their neckties so they all would know each other.

At last, suspicions were aroused and vigilantes caught Plummer and gave him one of the most deserved 'necktie parties' in Western history.

'Bleeding Kansas'

Far worse than anything that happened on the gold-fields was the situation in Kansas and Missouri before the Civil War, and certain events after the war were caused by the savagery rampant along the border in the 1850s.

In that bloody decade, murderous pro- and anti-slavery gangs battled it out with each other, providing excellent training for some nightmarish

John Brown.

tactics in the Civil War. The names of the two gangs were the Kansas 'Freesoilers' and the Missouri 'Border Ruffians'. The pro-slavery Border Ruffians were the more murderous of the two killer packs, looting and burning in Kansas and killing all who dared attempt to save their families. However, the Kansans had a ferocious champion in the person of the fanatical John Brown.

One night in 1856, Lawrence, Kansas was looted by Border Ruffians who, however, did not kill anyone. John Brown – some say to settle a personal score – led a revenge raid on log cabins at Pottawatomie Creek. Armed with broadswords and guns, they dragged five harmless farmers from their homes and murdered them. Despite attempts to 'prove' the martyr-to-be free from guilt, one of the gang later clinched Brown's guilt.

Inevitably, the Civil War as it affect-

Above: John Brown, fanatic.

Opposite page: A lynching in Laramie, Wyoming, in 1868, with three men 'jerked to Jesus'.

ed the area was an extension of the horrors that had gone before. The first atrocity occurred in September 1861 when General James Lane pursued General Sterling Price on a retaliatory raid into Missouri, punishing Price's alleged helpers. His men were soon looting and murdering, while in Osceola nine men were shot after being 'court-martialled' and the town was destroyed.

The most notorious guerilla leader, William Clarke Quantrill, was provoked to side with the South by this atrocity and picked a ruthless band to serve him. It included the notorious 'Bloody Bill' Anderson, the Youngers, and Frank James. On August 21st, 1863 they avenged Osceola by an assault on Lawrence, Kansas, with 400 men, destroying it and killing some 150.

Frank James joined 'Bloody Bill's' band with the latter started his own outfit. Anderson was a walking arsenal at times, carrying up to eight revolvers and a hatchet in his belt, as well as two pistols in his saddle holsters. Believing that his sister's death was attributable to Union troops, he carried a silken cord, adding a knot to it for every Yankee he exterminated.

Arch Clement, one of his boys, may have killed up to 300 men before he was 20. He is said to have burnt men at the stake, and he took scalps.

The James Boys

The defeat of the South added extra bitterness which was to cause yet more violence, and nowhere were feelings more enflamed than in the North-western counties of the State of Missouri. In one of them, Clay County, Frank James had been born in 1844 and Jesse in 1847. How much of their later career can be ascribed to the savage border warfare they had taken part in and how much to their own lethal character defects cannot be determined.

Jesse's wounds were so serious in 1865 that he nearly died. Most of his surviving companions were paroled by the victors, but some had no intention of living peacefully, even if those of their neighbours who had fought for the Union would have let them.

On February 13th, 1866, the Clay County Savings Association Bank in Liberty, Missouri, was robbed of $57,000 in bonds and currency and between $5,000 and $15,000 in gold coin. The robbers were 12 or 13 strong, three acting as lookouts, while most of the population were being entertained by a trial in the local Justice Court. On their way out of town, a totally wanton killing occurred, young George 'Jolly' Wymore being shot as he stood on the opposite side of the street.

Surprisingly perhaps, armed bank robbery was a new development.

Opposite page: Bloody Bill Anderson, a notorious guerilla leader in the Civil War, who helped 'train' Frank and Jesse James.

Below: A bearded Jesse James with an unknown friend.

James

Apart from a daring raid out of Canada in banks in St. Alban's, Vermont, led by a Confederate officer in 1864, such a crime was new, and, of course, the Confederate raid was decidedly patriotic.

There is no proof that the James boys were at Liberty, but James experts like Jeff Burton are prepared to state that Frank was probably there and Jesse may have been. The raid's leader may have been the notorious Arch Clement, much admired by young Jesse, and one of the few guerillas not given a parole. A grim feature of the incident was the gang's marksmanship, for any one of the four bullets that tore into the unfortunate Wymore could have killed him.

Nearby Lexington suffered next, the gang failing to take more than $2,000 because the vault could not be forced. The robberies continued, without Clement after another attempt on Lexington where he was killed in an ambush. The James boys took part in some of the raids, but as yet only members of the murderous teams.

The question arises as to how so many of the local population sympathized with the gangs, for it was now peacetime and local money was being taken. The reason was that many farmers whose land had been ravaged by both sides needed money to get back on their feet. When they discovered that the bankers, whatever their politics, hated parting with money except at exorbitant rates of interest, it naturally made them somewhat sympathetic to those who extracted money directly from these extortionists.

Another significant fact was that the robbers never left any bonds behind, since there was no problem in redeeming them.

Not all the raids were successful — several robbers were caught and lynched after a raid at Richmond. Cole

Left: An unusual setting for a hanging in Kansas.

Right: Mrs. Zerelda Samuel, the redoubtable mother of the James Boys.

Younger, aged 24, was a new recruit who first saw service with four others at Russellville, Kentucky, in 1868. $14,000 was taken, but not without incident. Younger held a gun at the elderly president's head, but he bravely broke away with no more than a creased head, and soon the local citizens were aroused to action. Though the five escaped, one of them, George Shepherd, called to one onlooker: 'You needn't be particular about seeing my face so well you'd remember it again.' He later served three years for his foolishness.

Hopes that Jesse would be a new man after being baptized at the Kearney Baptist Church were dashed when the Davies County Savings Bank at Gallatin was robbed in December 1869. A cashier was shot dead, an unlikely excuse being that he looked like the Yankee officer who had killed Bloody Bill Anderson back in the good old days.

The brothers only just got out of town, Jesse clutching on to Frank, his own horse having bolted. When the horse was later identified, the boys found themselves in print – and were branded as outlaws. With $3,000 on his head, Jesse wrote sadly about the injustice of it all to the *Kansas City Times*. As the editor was a staunch Confederate, Jesse now had a good platform, the paper spreading the myth of two persecuted peace-loving boys.

The James Gang as such dates from 1871, the James-Younger gang from April 29th, 1872, when a mere $1,500 was taken from a Columbia bank, and a cashier being murdered in the process. The next year trains were added to their repertoire, train robbery having been invented by the Reno

The James Gang's raid on Northfield, Minnesota's, First National Bank in 1876 was a disaster, thanks to the valour of its citizens.

ROBBERS KILLED
Clell Miller
Bill Stiles, alias
Chadwell
Charlie Pitts
WOUNDED & CAPTURED
Cole Younger
Jim Younger
Bob Younger

ESCAPED
Jesse James
Frank James

brothers back in 1866. At their height, the James-Younger organization had several gangs and the public was becoming distinctly hostile to them — at which point a botched exploit by Pinkerton detectives changed the prevailing mood decisively.

Allan Pinkerton (see page 138) had already lost some men to the gang. He was finding it virtually impossible to get an undercover agent into Clay County, the heart of James country, but one Jack Ladd, posing as a farm hand, finally managed it and a force of Pinkerton men and local detectives surrounded the house of Mrs. Zerelda Samuel, Jesse's formidable mother. A metal object was tossed into the cabin, a flare according to the Law, a grenade according to the James supporters. Whatever the truth, it was shovelled into the fire and exploded. Jesse's 9-year-old stepbrother was killed and his mother lost her right forearm. She at once went to war, stating that her boys had not even been at home that night, and soon far too many Missourians saw the dangerous brothers as martyrs. The Pinkerton campaign failed, but their tactics made the gang seek out more distant targets, at one of which Nemesis awaited them.

This was Northfield, Minnesota, the target being the First National Bank, the date – after careful planning – being September 7th, 1876. There were determined men in Northfield who, when they realized what was happening, armed themselves and attacked the invaders. Frank and Jesse barely escaped with their lives, Frank being hit in the leg. Cole Younger was hit in the shoulder, his brother Jim in the face, and Bob Younger in the thigh. However, only two of the eight-strong gang were dead. In the event, only Jesse and Frank reached home, though a bullet from one of a posse went through both of them. The three Youngers were rounded up, all badly wounded. Charlie Pitts was killed. Bob Younger died in prison in 1889, his brothers being released in 1901. Cole was to team up with Frank James lecturing about the evils of crime.

After Northfield, Jesse laid low for three years, Frank for longer, but a train robbery in 1879, with one of the gang later revealing the leader's name,

led to a new manhunt for Jesse, complete with big rewards. He had become a political issue by now and there were behind-the-scenes discussions between bandits and officials. Finally, Governor Crittenden of Missouri enlisted one of Jesse's own gang to kill him. So it came about that on April 3rd, 1882, Jesse, alias J.D. Howard, and living with his wife and two children in St. Joseph, Missouri, was shot in the head by Ford while he was standing on a chair dusting a picture on the wall. Ford was promptly pardoned after trial, but was still reviled

Above: Bob Ford, killer of Jesse James.

121

by many as a traitor until he, too, was killed in 1892. Yet the 'dirty little coward who shot Mr. Howard' as the ballad has it, was no more a traitor than the unsavoury Jesse had been, for he had too often quarreled with, informed on, and lied against those who had sheltered him and ridden with him.

Brother Frank later gave himself up and was miraculously convicted of nothing – Minnesotan lawmen could not get at him. Apart from his double-act with Cole Younger, he admitted people to the James home for 50 cents and only fired guns as the starter at local fairs.

The Daltons

The West spawned other gangs, the best known of them, Butch Cassidy and the Wild Bunch, taking their historical place in the final chapter of this book. The gang that came to the most spectacularly melodramatic end was the Daltons, who were kinsmen of the Youngers. Their home was Coffeyville, Kansas, and four of the 15 children of Lewis and Adeline Dalton became famous, Grat, Bill, Bob and Emmett. Their brother Frank was one of 'Hanging Judge' Parker's deputies but was killed in Indian Territory in 1887. Bob and Grat were lawmen for a while, Bill seemed to settle down and Emmett worked on a ranch, but the lure of crime proved too strong. Soon, they were among the many outlaws that infested the unfortunate Indian Territory.

Their success went to their heads and they planned to rob two banks at once in their own home town. With Dick Broadhead and Tim Evans, but without brother Bill, they rode into town on October 5th, 1892, only to find that the street between the banks was under repair. They had to leave their horses half a block away.

The ill-planned venture was made more fatuous by their incompetent disguises – false beards and absurd-looking moustaches. Bob and Emmett were recognized by a passer-by who saw them taking $20,000 from the First National Bank. He rushed into the square shouting: 'The Daltons! The Daltons!' Instantly, the townspeople either grabbed their own

guns or borrowed them from a store.

Meanwhile, Emmett, Grat, Broadwell and Evans were in trouble at the Condon Bank, the brave teller having told the would-be robbers that there was a time lock on the vault that could not be opened. With more time wasted, the enraged citizens were ready for action and, as the gang tried to reach their horses, a major gunfight commenced.

When it had ended, four brave citizens were dead and, except for Emmett, all the invaders were dead or dying. The surviving Dalton got life imprisonment but only served 14 years. He later acted as an adviser for Western films in Hollywood and wrote about law and order, dying of natural causes in 1937.

Policing the Cowtowns

The senior lawmen in the West were US marshals, appointed by the President and approved of by Congress before overseeing states and territories. The deputies they appointed worked with local lawmen, and in fact might already be peace officers. They dealt with Federal crimes, including those committed on reservations. Town marshals were appointed locally and they engaged a number of deputies. A town marshal's job, the occasional shoot-out apart, included seeing that brothels did not become too disorderly and shooting stray dogs for a small fee. The sheriff was in charge of a county and had an under-sheriff and deputies working for him. Few made a full career out of the job of lawman, not least because the pay was poor. Only the very fortunate sheriff received $500 a month, a deputy perhaps less than $70 a month. What must be stressed is that lawmen could expect help from citizens, the townspeople of Northfield and Coffeyville no exceptions. The otherwise magnificent movie, *High Noon*, is historically inaccurate for leaving the marshal alone to fight his enemies.

The cowtowns – Abilene, Dodge City, Wichita, Newton and the rest – were the most famous stages for confrontation between Law and Disorder. It was inevitable that after the long trail drive, the cowboy, having enjoyed a bath and thrown away his

Right: Bob and Grat Dalton, dying or dead, after their disastrous raid on Coffeyville, Kansas in 1892. The Daltons in feeble disguises, attacked their own home town – and paid the penalty.

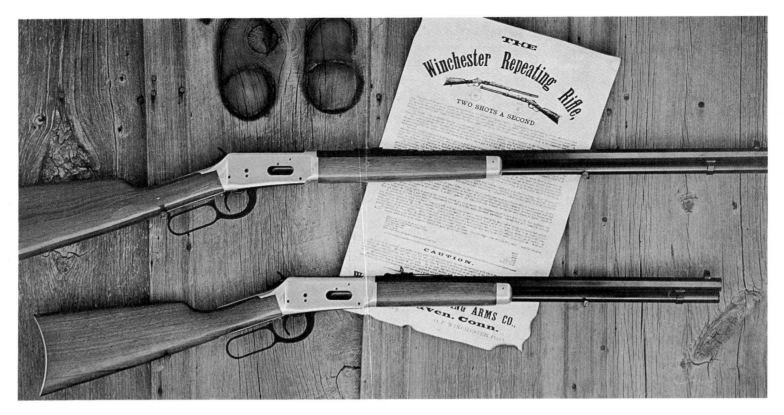

verminous clothes, wanted action, which, before capable lawmen were in charge, was liable to involve shooting up the town. A weak lawman was likely to be chased out of the locality, and, as has been noted, the fact that most lawmen were Northerners, hardly made for popularity. True, very few cowboys were a match for a professional gunfighter within or without the law, but a horde of pistol-toting Texans naturally scared the average citizen.

Abilene, the first great cowtown, set the pattern, and by 1869 was almost a Texan town in the cattle season. The boys set fire to parts of it, including a new jail, and enjoyed riding into saloons. Shooting at passers-by added to the anarchy.

In 1870, Mayor T.C. Henry hired a large, handsome lawman named Tom Smith to tame the Texans. Tame them he did using two weapons that startled them – his sledgehammer fists. He once said: 'Anyone can bring in a dead man, but to my way of thinking a good officer is the one that brings them in alive.'

It was Smith who first made cow-boys hand over their guns to the bartender 'to keep until you want to go out of camp', or, as many a Western has it, 'Park yer shootin' irons on the bar'. The city fathers realized they had an asset and paid him well, while he

continued to ride around town on his grey stallion Silverheels, the two pearl-handled Colts in their holsters, unused, except occasionally to beat some sense into a would-be shootist. As for the rides through town, Smith said that a man on a moving horse was harder for a drunk to hit than a lone man patrolling on foot. Three failed assassination attempts proved his point.

Having survived Abilene's busiest season in triumph, Tom Smith the man who may have once been a New York cop, was murdered out of season by two settlers. Abilene gave him the

Above: A Winchester advertisement of 1966 to celebrate the centenary of the Model of 1866.

Below: Colt .44 New Model Army revolver of 1860. Though Sam Colt died in 1862, his firm goes marching on.

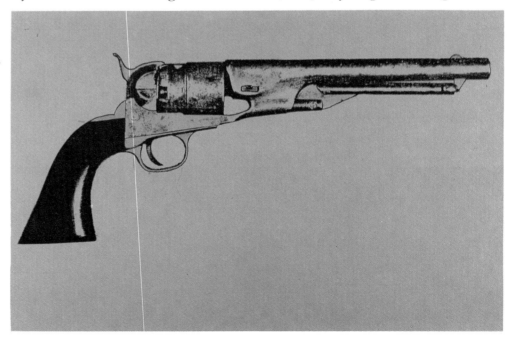

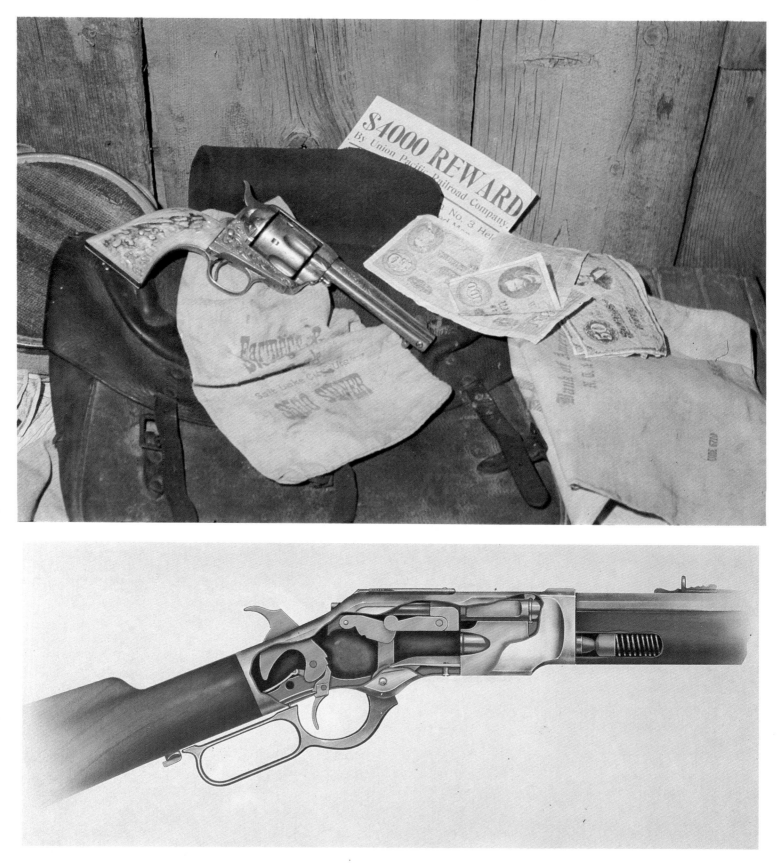

greatest funeral that the town has ever witnessed.

In 1871, the City Council hired a man destined to be remembered as perhaps the most notable gunfighter of them all, James Butler 'Wild Bill' Hickok, the 'Prince of Pistoleers'.

Born in Illinois in 1837, he was said to have killed more than a hundred men, a rumour helped along by his own Frontier powers of exaggeration. He actually told the young H.M. Stanley, later the great explorer but then a reporter: 'I have killed over a hundred, a long ways over . . . I never killed one man without good cause.' Joseph G. Rosa, the leading authority on Hickok, has discovered seven

Top: The Colt .45 single action Army model owned by Harvey Logan (Kid Curry) of the Wild Bunch, with his gunbelt and holster.

Above: A cutaway drawing by Terry Hadler showing the finely designed rapid action loading and repeating mechanism of the immortal Winchester '73.

substantiated slayings!

Hickok went to Kansas in his teens in 1856 to buy land for his family to farm, but found himself in the midst of the bitter Border wars. After spells as a lawman and stagecoach driver, he took part in the Civil War on the Union side, serving as a wagonmaster, scout, courier and spy. His meeting with Stanley came after the war when he was serving as an army scout.

Custer's wife Libbie was one of his admirers, giving this description of him in *Boots and Saddles*:

Physically, he was a delight to look upon. Tall, lithe, and free in every motion, he rode and walked as if every muscle was perfection, and the careless swing of his body as he moved seemed perfectly in keeping with the man, the country, the time in which he lived.

His reputation was considerable by the time he was appointed Marshal of Abilene in 1871, not least in Hays, Kansas. In July 1870, he returned to the town – where he had once killed

Below: Dead soldiers at Hays City, Kansas, in 1873. One David Roberts did the deed outside Cy Goddard's saloon.

two men while acting as acting sheriff of Ellis County – to look up some friends. He was set upon by drunken cavalrymen, member's of his friend Custer's Seventh Cavalry, and shot two of them. The circumstances are disputed, but one of the troopers died and Wild Bill had to leave town quickly.

He reached Abilene with an unequalled reputation as a gunfighter. No longer did he wear buckskins, but dressed fashionably. In his belt were twin Colt Navy revolvers, butts for-ward, and he rightly took good care of himself, so great was his reputation. Back in 1865 in Springfield, Missouri, he had killed a man named Tutt on the town square in one of the few shootouts that bore some resemblance to Hollywood's formal gunfights at high noon. He had even swung round on friends of Tutt's and uttered the immortal words: 'Put up your shootin'-irons, or there'll be more dead men here.' But now in Abilene he rightly, as Joseph Rosa has put it, 'avoided bright lights and dark alley-ways'. This was Abilene's last and greatest season as a cowtown, and he survived.

The most notorious episode in his reign came near the end of the season on October 5th. There were still some Texans in town; Hickok noted around 50 having a good time in the saloons. He was told that people were being forced to buy the boys drinks after being carried into the saloons. Wanting no trouble, Hickok, according to one version of what happened, bought some Texans drinks after they prom-

ised not to use their guns.

About 9 pm, he was having a drink with his close friend Mike Williams in the Novelty Theatre when he heard a shot from outside the Alamo Saloon. Telling Williams to stay put, he crossed to the Alamo and found a crowd of armed Texans, with gambler Philip Coe, pistol in hand, at their head. When Hickok asked who had fired the shot, Coe said that he had – at a dog. Having been warned that Coe was out to get him, the Marshal of Abilene was not convinced.

Tension had been building for a long time between the two men, and

Below: An 1867 coloured engraving of Wild Bill Hickok.

128

now Hickok was particularly angry for the Texans were blatantly defying the ordinance against firearms in town. He told them to disarm and leave Abilene, and, as he spoke, Coe pointed his pistol at him. Wild Bill drew his own Navies and fired, but just as he did so, someone came between them. The interloper was hit by both bullets and fell into the street, for the confrontation had occurred at the front entrance of the Alamo.

Coe had fired twice, one shot ripping Hickok's coat tail, the other going between his legs. Hickok shot Coe twice in the stomach. One of Coe's shots hit an onlooker and, as the man fell, Hickok turned and shouted: 'If any of you want the balance of these pills, come and get them.' As the Texans stood motionless, Hickok roared an order at them to get out of town and the place was soon almost empty.

The Stock Exchange Bank at Caldwell, Kansas.

Hickok registered that Coe was mortally wounded, then saw to his horror who the interloper was. It was his friend Mike Williams, dead.

Weeping, he carried Williams into the Alamo and laid him on a billiard table, then, like a man berserk, he raged through the saloons still open in Abilene and drove everyone he found out of them. Rumours were rife that Coe had been shot in the back, but although Hickok's employers dis-

believed them, they had already had enough of their city being a cowtown (though it had made them rich) and decided to ask the cattlemen to go elsewhere in 1872. Hickok was not sacked, as his enemies alleged. There was simply no longer a job for him. *The Chronicle* spoke for the majority of citizens when it praised his work in Abilene.

He had less than five years to live. Some of that time was spent, not very

happily, as an actor with his friend Buffalo Bill Cody, but he headed West again, and 1876 found him in Deadwood in the Black Hills of Dakota. There, he was shot through the back of the head in a saloon by a hired killer named Jack McCall as he was playing cards. A jury set the killer free, but a legal trial condemned McCall to death and he was hanged on March 1st, 1877.

Hickok lies buried a few feet away

Left; Bat Masterson, lawman, gunfighter and gambler. He finally became a New York sportswriter, dying at his desk.

Below: A group of Texas Rangers, with John R. Hughes (seated right), who was to become a legendary Frontier lawman.

from the burial place of Calamity Jane, who used to boast that she had been his lover, even his wife. There is no shred of truth in her story, but Martha Jane Cannary, as she was probably called, was never one to worry about that. She does seem to have met him, however. Her character was summed up while she was providing comfort for Union Pacific railroad builders in the 1860s. She was characterized as a 'good-hearted hussy, hard as nails'. Space does not permit details of the various versions she gave as to how she acquired her nickname. She was once locked in the closet of a brothel because her language was too foul.

Other towns took over from Abilene, including Newton where, so a writer in the Wichita *Tribune* stated, 'You may see young girls not over sixteen drinking whiskey, smoking, cursing and swearing.'

The town of Caldwell was served by an excellent marshal named Henry Newton Brown, who married a local girl and neither drank nor swore nor chewed tobacco. No one knew that he had had a 'past' in the Lincoln County War, but even if they had, he was still a paragon in Caldwell. Alas, in May 1884 the bad news broke that he and three others had tried to rob the bank at Medicine Lodge, murdering two, but failing to get any money, the valiant cashier managing to lock the vault before he expired. The quartet were never tried, a mob shooting Brown and stringing up his three friends. Yet he had been the best lawman in Caldwell's history. The only explanation can be that greed overcame him.

Ellsworth, too, had typical cowtown troubles, some of them due to Yorkshire-born Ben Thompson, a master of triggernometry. Gambling was his main interest, though he later became a lawman in Austin, Texas, where his reputation helped promote peace. For quite a time he was forgiven for getting drunk and shooting at street lamps, but finally his behaviour was too blatant, and, after a

133

gunfight with an old enemy, he had to retire. He was murdered in 1884.

Wichita's stormy history began when the railroad arrived in 1872. Wyatt Earp was there for a time, as an efficient officer, rather than the superman of legend. The 'superman' was one S.M. Tucker, a lawyer.

The Texans were at their wildest when someone sounded the police alarm. Armed citizens always came running, to be faced, on one occasion, by William 'Hurricane Bill' Martin and the 'Texas Gang' who were disturbing everyone's peace with pistols. Lawman William Smith was not the man for the situation, but Tucker was. Who did the marshal want arrested? was his question and the lawman pointed at 'Hurricane' Bill. Tucker cocked his shotgun, aimed it at Bill and told him to drop his guns. Bill was impressed enough to shrug his shoulders and say: 'I guess you can have me!' Moments later he and his cronies were being marched to jail.

The 'Queen of the Cowtowns' was Dodge City, which got its title in 1874, its best-known lawman being Bat Masterson, two of whose brothers also served on the force, although Bat was actually Sheriff of Ford County. Ed Masterson was shot in a ferocious gunfight against two opponents and was given a fine funeral, so great was his reputation. Bat, who enjoyed telling tall tales, and who never contradicted ludicrous legends about the number of his killings, died at the sports desk of a New York paper in 1921.

Dodge City remained a cowtown until the trail cattle industry ended in 1885. Books and films give the impression of a death toll in the cowtowns that ran into many thousands. A revised total in Robert Dykstra's *The Cattle Towns* (1968) claimed that only 45 killings occurred between 1870–85, which put the matter in perspective. However, since then others have suggested that, especially in Newton and Dodge, the total was much higher, if nowhere near the thousands of legend.

The Texas Rangers

The best known group of lawmen in the West were the Texas Rangers. Canadians and Britons are entitled to claim that the Mounties, founded in 1873 as the North-West Mounted Police, were as fine a force, but the Canadian West was less populated and 'wild', while most Indians trusted the men in their scarlet coats.

Like the Mountie, the Texas Ranger was expected to tackle any challenge single-handed if necessary, hence the classic story of the mayor who found himself with a riot on his hands and telegraphed 'Urgently need a company of rangers' to their headquarters in Austin.

Two days later, a train reached the troubled West Texas town and out of it emerged a man with a Winchester, a Colt and a bag. Startled, the mayor asked: 'Where's the rest of 'em?'

'There's just me,' the man replied.

The mayor objected: 'I asked for a company!'

'Why so you did,' said the Ranger, 'but there's only one riot, ain't there?' 'One riot, one ranger' became a memorable part of Texas history.

There were rangers in Texas before the Americans rebelled against the Mexicans. When the first settlers arrived from the U.S.A. in the 1820s, the Mexicans raised rangers to protect them from the Comanches. There were 15 of them and, later, the American leader Stephen Austin, raised ten more. They were first called Texas Rangers during the Texas Revolution of 1835–36. One hundred and fifty were raised in 1835, and all were expected to provide their own horses and survive on $1.25 a day. A legendary hero of the early days was Captain John 'Jack' Coffee Hays, he and his men with their new Colt five-shooters, tracking down hostile Indians and white badmen alike.

In 1865, the defeated Texans were deprived of their Rangers by the victors. After a spell with the Union Army responsible for peace on the Frontier, the Texas State Police were put in charge, a much hated force mainly of ex-slaves. Governor F.J. Davis meant well, but the force was controversial and did anything but foster good feeling. In 1874, the Rangers were reactivated.

Major John B. Jones commanded the Frontier Battalion, which fought Indians and quelled feuds, while Captain McNelly's Special Force sup-

Right: A cartoon of the 1860s, showing a heavily armed, heavily bearded Texas Ranger.

Overleaf: Guns and badges used by Texas Rangers, now in the Dogie Wright Collection.

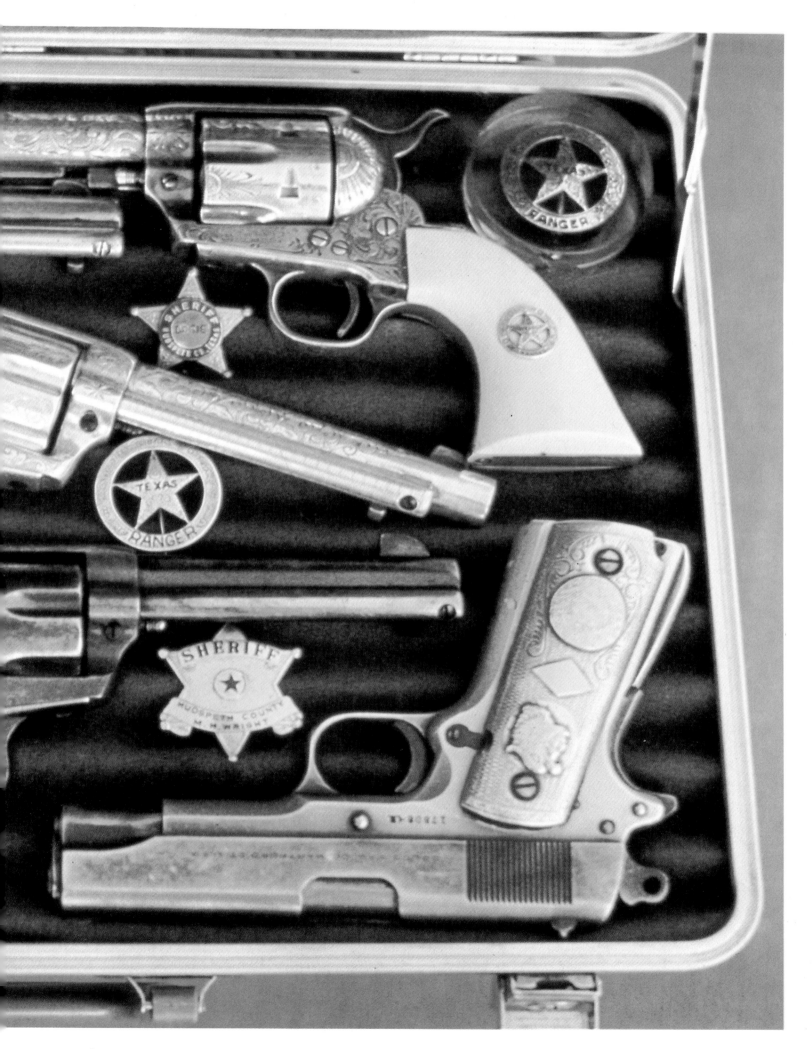

pressed lawlessness along the border. The greatest modern Ranger was Frank Hamer, born in 1884, who was brought back from retirement to track down Bonnie and Clyde. The film of that name, brilliant as it was, libelled him grossly in the totally false scene where he was captured and photographed, as well as in the finale when the pair were killed. The idea of Hamer being captured by such a man, Hamer who made himself as much like an Indian as a boy, who tamed wild border towns, was wounded 17 times, left for dead on four occasions, and took part in more gunfights than any other Ranger, is ludicrous. A legend in his lifetime, he died of natural causes in 1955.

Pinkertons and Others

Private enterprise battled to fight Western crime along with the official forces, the best known example being the famous detective agency founded by Scottish born Allan Pinkerton. He started before the Civil War, uncovering a plot to murder Abraham Lincoln soon after his election.

In the Civil War, he set up the North's secret service, but repeatedly exaggerated the South's strength. The Union commander, McClennan, who was anyway loath to attack, believed the reports and was finally sacked. Pinkerton's influence waned. He was not at hand when Lincoln was assassinated and always lamented the fact, believing, with some reason, that he could have protected him.

After the war came national fame, despite the failure with the James gang. The Pinkerton 'Rogues Gallery', complete with details of criminals and their photographs, undoubtedly helped tame the West. Other agencies helped, notably Wells Fargo and Union Pacific, both of which employed determined detectives and equally determined guards on stagecoaches and wagons. The finest detective employed by Wells Fargo was William Hume, though, ironically, he had most trouble from one of the gentlest badmen in Western history.

This was 'Black Bart' — real name, Charles E. Bolton — who robbed stagecoaches without harming anyone

and signed himself 'Black Bart the PO 8'. After his third hold-up – he was to achieve 28 – he left four lines of verse which made him a Western immortal:

I've labored long and hard for bread
For honor and for riches
But on my corns, too long you've trod
You fine haired Sons of Bitches.

His luck finally ran out for, as well as being wounded, he dropped a handkerchief at the scene of a holdup and on it was a laundry mark, F.X.O.7. One of the detectives on the case was Harry Morse. After checking many towns, he struck lucky in San Francisco. The handkerchief belonged to a Charles E. Bolton, a mining man, so he claimed without success. However, as he handed back most of his loot and had never harmed anyone, he received just six years.

The Taming of Indian Territory

As has been described, the Five Civilized Tribes, were driven westwards in the 1830s. The Civil War split them and constant trail drives through their territory hardly made for peace. Also by the 1860s, many other tribes had been driven into Indian Territory, then bigger than what would become the state of Oklahoma. Yet the worst change – since their forced emigration – was yet to come. Indian Territory became a paradise for badmen.

In 1870, there were some 50,000 Indians there, mostly from the five tribes. Law was in the hands of a single judge and his small band of lawmen, their headquarters finally being at Fort Smith 100 yards from Indian Territory. Fortunately for the Law, a great judge appeared in 1875, Isaac Parker, who served for 21 years. He is remembered as the Hanging Judge, but was in fact the Indians' friend.

His deputies were ill-paid and some had criminal records, but they were the best he could get. They had three notable leaders, Heck Thomas, William Tilghman and Chris Madsen, and it was this trio, known as the 'Oklahoma Guardsmen', who, with white and Indian police, tamed the turbulent territory. In the case of Ned Christie, a

Right: Frank Hamer, the greatest modern Ranger, who was grossly mischaracterized in the film Bonnie and Clyde. *He spanned the old frontier days and newer types of crime.*

Cherokee blacksmith before becoming an outlaw, the taming including dynamite and a cannon, used on his stronghold.

Parker's methods shocked the ignorant in the East, and sharp young lawyers, combined with reversals of his decisions by the Supreme Court, gradually curbed his necessary powers. Only the worst criminals were likely to hang, though it is only fair to state that Parker's mass hangings, vividly portrayed in *True Grit*, created understandable hostility towards him – in the East and among the criminal classes! Only after his death was his worth finally realized. The Indians had always known it. A Creek chief, one of many Indian mourners, brought wild flowers to his funeral.

Parker had lived to see the career of the Territory's most notorious badman ended by Heck Thomas. This was Bill Doolin, who had the good luck to miss the disastrous raid on Coffeyville, staged by his Dalton cousins.

Affable and able, he led a successful gang of train and bank robbers. They knew Oklahoma well, had a hideout in a cave, and many friends, especially in Ingalls. Bill married the daughter of the town's Methodist minister. Generous with other people's money, he appears also to have been unique among Western badmen in that he actually gave some to the poor.

His hideout beside the Cimarron River was accidently found by Bill Tilghman in 1895. He also found eight rifles pointing at him which he wisely pretended not to see. Legend has it that Doolin ordered the lawmen left alone because he was 'too good a man to be shot in the back'. More likely, Doolin ordered his men not to kill Tilghman, who was very popular and whose death would have attracted a huge posse.

Tilghman finally caught Doolin at Eureka Springs, Arkansas, where the outlaw was treating his rheumatism. Disguised as a minister, the lawman ordered a bath then pulled a gun on Doolin, who could only surrender, especially as he assumed that the marshal was not alone.

The arrest caused a sensation and Doolin was driven round Guthrie, the capital, in a cab packed with marshals,

Left: Black Bart, the non-violent, poetical hold-up artist and snappy dresser.

Right: Georgia-born Heck Thomas, who helped to tame Indian Territory, later Oklahoma. He died in bed in 1912.

to the delight of thousands of admirers. He was given a fine meal, then jailed, but soon escaped, leading 13 other prisoners to freedom.

It seems that Doolin wanted to give up crime and settle in Mexico or Canada, not least because an old leg injury was troubling him. It was not to be. A posse led by Thomas tracked him down and when Doolin went for his gun, Thomas killed him.

Tilghman was the only one of the great trio of Oklahoma guardsmen to die in action – in Cromwell, Oklahoma in 1924 when he was over 70. Cromwell was a wild oil town, and one night, hearing a shot, Tilghman went on to the street just as he would have done in his young days in Dodge City. He seized his man and had an onlooker take his weapon away. But the man, a drunken prohibition officer, had a second weapon and killed the elderly lawman.

Bill Tilghman had once said: 'I want to go out in the smoke and die with my boots on', which he did.

Gunsmoke on the Range

Range wars, the background or foreground of so many Westerns, saw the old tradition of feuding and fighting in earlier Wests carried across the Missouri. Two stand out, the Lincoln County War and the Johnson County War, though a third, Arizona's Pleasant Valley War in the 1880s, carried the annihilation of the Grahams and Tewksburys to such a pitch that Zane Gray's fictional version of events was rightly called *To The Last Man*. Although it is no longer accepted that the 'war' was a straightforward cattlemen versus sheepmen confrontation, which was triggered off the day that a cry went up from ranch to ranch, 'The Tewksburys are driving sheep over the rim of Mogollons', the highlights remain unchallenged.

They included a gun battle at the Tewksbury cabin, which was halted after several hours when hogs began to eat two bodies outside the cabin and John Tewksbury's widow rushed out

screaming that she must bury them. The shooting did not immediately cease, but died as the men were shamed, starting again as soon as the widow returned to the cabin. It only ended when a posse arrived. The war lasted from 1886–92, when there was little blood left to spill. But there was to be a sensational aftermath.

The young widow of the last of the Grahams entered the court where John Rhodes, her husband's suspected killer, was on trial. From her umbrella she drew his six-shooter, pressed it to Rhodes' back and fired. The gun failed to go off and before she could try again, pandemonium broke out and she was rushed out of court by her friends.

Although it ranks as a range war, the Lincoln County War was basically a lethal struggle for the economic and political control of Lincoln County, New Mexico. In the county seat, the small town of Lincoln, three Irishmen, James Dolan, Laurence Murphy and John Riley, and a German named

142

Emil Fritz, built a power base that embraced most of the county. Their headquarters was the main store, known as The House. Their cattle were sold to nearby Fort Stanton and the Mescalero Apache Reservation; William Brady, the sheriff of Lincoln, was their creature. Better still, they had close links with corrupt politicians and businessmen, the 'Santa Fe Ring'.

The war broke out in 1878, by which time Fritz was dead and Dolan semi-retired. The House was loathed by the ordinary people of the county, who were underpaid for their cattle, forced to buy expensive goods, and in danger of losing their land. Meanwhile, the Apache failed to get their full rations, and rustling and murders steadily increased. The military seemed not to notice, having been blinded by The House as to what was going on.

Against The House was cattle king John Chisum, whose cattle were being stolen and who wanted its contracts to supply beef. His main allies were Canadian-born Alexander McSween, a lawyer, and an ambitious young English businessman, John Tunstall. Backed by Chisum and helped by his father's wealth, he opened his own store near the Murphy one. McSween was his partner. The local people naturally preferred the new store.

Tension increased when first Dolan had McSween arrested for alleged

Above: John Graham, a victim of the ferocious Graham-Tewksbury feud in Arizona, known as the Pleasant Valley War.

Left: Bill Tilghman, another great lawman, pictured in 1898. Years after his famous days in Oklahoma he was killed by a drunken prohibition officer when he was 70 in 1924.

Right: English-born businessman John Tunstall, whose murder in 1878 sparked off the Lincoln County War.

embezzlement and actually had Chisum in prison for a time for alleged debts. Gunsmoke was inevitable.

It came on February 18th, 1878 when Tunstall was murdered. A youth whom he had befriended and who was working for him under the name of William Bonney is said to have sworn an oath of vengeance over his grave. Born Henry McCarty in 1859, he is best known to history as Billy the Kid.

Tunstall's foreman, Dick Brewer, who, with Billy, had been unable to save their boss, now raised a party of 11 'Regulators', armed with warrants, who captured two of their enemies and killed them while 'resisting arrest'. Meanwhile, The House was after McSween, Dolan getting the 'truth' to the territorial governor in Santa Fe. But the next round went to McSween, his men killing Brady and a deputy after an ambush by Tunstall's store.

There followed a heroic last stand. The Regulators, seeking out every opponent, not just those who were present at Tunstall's death, came across Andrew 'Buckshot' Roberts at Blazer's Mill on the Mescalero Reservation. Roberts, whose nickname came from an old shoulder wound which made him shoot from the hip, was seen at the Agency by his old friend, Frank Coe, who urged him to surrender. The rest of the Regulators were finishing a meal inside the Agency.

The Regulators began to leave the building, and Frank Coe warned him to surrender. It was too late even if the game old man had wanted to. His enemies were some 15 feet (4.5 m) away from him, including one Charlie Bowdre, who ordered: 'Throw up your arms or you are a dead man.'

Instead, Roberts raised his rifle and fired, and so did Bowdre. Roberts was hit in the stomach, his own bullet shooting off Bowdre's gun belt, then mangling Frank's cousin George Coe's trigger finger.

Roberts retreated along a wall as the Regulators started firing at him. He hit one of them in the lung, then Billy the Kid rushed at him and was winded by his carbine. He missed his shot.

Roberts reached Dr. Blazer's office. He had no bullets left, but found the doctor's Springfield 45–60 and a supply of ammunition. He put a mattress in front of a slightly open door, got down and began firing. The day grew hotter and so did the Regulators' tempers until Brewer crept to some logs near the sawmill and fired at the doorway. There was silence and he fired again; a split second later the top of his head was blasted off.

This great shot ended the battle. The Regulators had had enough and Roberts was buried the following day next to Dick Brewer.

The climax of the 'war' came in a five-day battle in Lincoln itself, which began when 50 McSween men hit town hoping to win it back. The first three days saw little real action, but Dolan had an ally in Colonel Dudley of Fort Stanton who sent all his officers save one, 30 men and artillery to help The House. The valiant Mrs. McSween tried to plead with the bigoted colonel but in vain. The McSween house was set on fire and Billy the Kid suggested that the survivors race towards the river. When the house was enveloped in flames, they began to run, Billy and one more reaching the river and only Mrs. McSween being spared.

A judge later vindicated the dead lawyer, whose wife's life was in danger as she searched what was left of her home. Such was her courage that her tormentors crept away in shame.

Now Dolan's men began a reign of terror in the county. Billy, whose career until Tunstall's murder had been by no means wild by Frontier standards, legends to the contrary, now became leader of a band of rustlers. Such was the anarchy in the county that General Lew Wallace of *Ben Hur* fame was sent to restore peace. Wanting to help balance several murder warrants against himself, Billy gave himself up to a surprised Wallace to testify against some of his enemies. Dolan was indicted – uselessly – and Billy was pardoned, though remaining technically under arrest. Then, when his pardon was questioned, he returned to crime until forced to surrender at Stinking Springs on December 23rd, 1880 to an old friend, Pat Garrett, Sheriff of Lincoln County.

Tried and convicted for murder, the *only* man to be so of all those who had fought in the War, he was put in

Right: The valiant Mrs. McSween who refused to be cowed by her husband's killers. She later became a successful rancher.

Sue E. McSween–Barber

the county jail, formerly the head-quarters of The House. On April 28th, 1881, when Garrett was away – legend has it that he was seeing to the building of Billy's scaffold – Billy escaped. The other prisoners were across the road at a restaurant, guarded by Robert Ollinger. Billy asked the other guard, J.W. Bell, to take him to the lavatory. Returning, he slipped the handcuffs from his slender hands and knocked Bell down with his chains. Then he shot him. A friend is thought to have concealed the gun in the privy during one of his visits to the Kid, slipping a note to him about the gun.

Billy raced to Garrett's office, seized his shotgun and went onto the balcony of the house, knowing that Ollinger would appear to find out about the shot. He killed him, shook hands with all and sundry and rode away with one leg still in chains. His feat was admired even by his enemies.

Garrett had his revenge on July 14th, 1881, when he found Billy at a friend's house at Fort Sumner. In the bedroom of rancher Pete Maxwell, Garrett waited, then killed the Kid, who at once became a Frontier immortal. He had not killed 21 men, one for every year of his life, as legend has it, but less than ten, the majority in conjunction with others. He was also not left-handed – a legend due to a photograph reproduced the wrong way round – nor was he insane. He was, however, ruthless, and, like Lincoln County for three bitter years, dangerous.

War in Johnson County

Johnson County was also dangerous a decade later. In the 1860s and 1870s, like much of Wyoming, it had seen bitter Indian warfare, but in the 1880s it became a cattleman's paradise. The calamities that hit the ranges in the mid-1880s have already been chronicled, but the surviving ranchers had learnt their lessons and were prospering. Despite barbed wire and the resulting outbreaks of violence, there was still open range left and many settlers came to 'squat on it' – most of them Americans or Western Europeans: *Heaven's Gate* with its hordes of eastern Europeans gave a

Left: This picture of Billy the Kid used to be reversed, hence the legend of his being a 'left-handed gun'.

Below: Billy the Kid shooting his way to freedom from Lincoln County Jail. It appeared in Sheriff Pat Garrett's allegedly authentic Life of Billy the Kid, *which was ghost-written by one Upson.*

Bottom: The death of Billy the Kid, as portrayed in The Authentic Life of Billy the Kid.

completely inaccurate portrayal.

It rightly stressed the anger and aggression of the cattle barons, however. They were not villains in the sense that The House and the Santa Fe Ring were in New Mexico, but as they talked things over in the exclusivity of their magnificent Cheyenne Club, as fine a club as any in New York, the threat to their well-being made them ruthless, with the power to be so. The Wyoming Stock Growers' Association, their organization, had some 100 members including the state governor and senators. A law allowed ranchers to claim any stray unbranded calf, allegedly aimed at rustlers, but with a sting in its tail whereby the strays were auctioned at such high prices that small cattlemen could not reclaim their beasts.

Detectives were hired by the association, and were paid so highly for 'rustlers' that injustice became rampant, while the chief detective was – though this was not known locally – a killer and robber turned lawman named Frank Canton. Before he was hired he had been sheriff of Johnson County and was already distrusted and even hated locally. He would become more so.

Above: 'Cattle Kate', an alleged rustler queen, whose real name was Ella Watson. She was a harmless whore who may have received some stolen cattle in lieu of money. She was hanged in 1889.

Left: Major Frank Wolcott, who led the Johnson County invaders pompously and unsuccessfully.

Top right: The KC Ranch where Nate Champion made his immortal last stand against an army of 'lawmen' in the Johnson County War.

Bottom right: The Cheyenne Club, as luxurious as any club in New York. In it the Johnson County War was planned.

The prelude to war happened outside Johnson County on the Sweetwater range. Beside the river lived small storekeeper Jim Averill and a whore named Ella Watson, who was sometimes paid in cattle by her cowboy friends. The local land was 'owned' by a rancher named Bothwell. In April 1889, Averill attacked cattle barons, in print, as land grabbers and speculators, fighting talk from a justice of the peace. In July he and Ella were hanged beside each other on a tree, after which Ella was slandered as a rustler queen, 'Cattle Kate'. No one was prosecuted, nor were they when, in June 1891, a horse-raiser named Waggoner was lynched.

The cabin of W.H. Hall beside the Powder River was the next target. At the time of the incident he was away, but Ross Gilbertson and Nate Champion were not. Nate, soon to be a Frontier immortal, drove the four interlopers off with his gun, wounding two of them – who were identified by their coats. One was arrested, jailed, and was soon over the state line. The denizens of the Cheyenne Club looked after their own.

The next two killings outraged the county, John Tisdale and Orley Jones

being men of unspotted reputations. Poor Tisdale was found dead in his wagon, Christmas toys for his children around him covered in blood. Frank Canton's horse was nearby. He was arrested – and released.

The settlers and small ranchers formed themselves into the Northern Wyoming Farmers' and Stock Grow-

ers' Association; their enemies drew up a 70-strong death list. Cattleman Major Frank Wolcott, who had been advocating an invasion of Johnson County, began planning one. The attackers should be hired from outside the state, all telegraph lines in Johnson County should be cut, then the 'army' should advance on Buffalo, the county

"THE INVADERS"
JOHNSON COUNTY CATTLE WAR. TAKEN AT Ft. D.A. RUSSELL
(FRANCIS E. WARREN) MAY 4th 1892.

NO 1 TON SMITH	NO 8 A.R. POWERS	NO 15 W.C. IRVINE
2 A.B. CLARKE	9 A.D. ADAMSON	16 BOB TISDALE
3 N. LESLIE	10 C.A. CAMPBELL	17 JOE ELLIOTT
4 E.H. WHITCOMB	11 FRANK LABERTEAUX	18 JOHN TISDALE
5 D. BROOKE	12 PHIL DUFRAN	19 SCOTT DAVIS
6 W.B. WALLACE	13 MAJOR WOLCOTT	20 FRED DE BILLIER
7 CHAS FORD	14 W.E. GUTHRIE	21 BEN MORRISON

NO 22 W.U. CLARKE	NO 29 J. BARLINGS	NO 36 JEFF MYNETT
23 L.H. PARKER	30 M.A. MC NALLY	37 BOB BARLINGS
24 TESCHMACHER	31 MIKE SHONSEY	38 S. SUTHERLAND
25 B.C. SCHULZE	32 DICK ALLEN	39 BUCK GARRETT
26 W.H. T. TABOR	33 FRED HESSE	40 G.R. TUCKER
27 J.J. GARRETT	34 FRANK CANTON	41 J.M. BENFORD
28 W.A. WILSON	35 Wm LITTLE	42 WILL ARMSTRONG

Top: A group photograph of the invaders of Wyoming's Johnson County, who wrongly claimed victory over the 'rustlers.'

Above: The scene is Rawlins County, Texas. Victims of the Dewey-Berry feud over water rights lie dead.

Left: A Colt Walker .44 percussion revolver dated 1847, one of a pair made for Captain Walker, Texas Rangers, who was influential in its design.

150

seat, where the wicked 'nesters' and rustlers lurked in strength. Target number one was Sheriff 'Red' Angus. He and all his men must be destroyed.

The acting governor of Wyoming was involved in the plan, as were the state senators, while Union Pacific laid on a special train to bring in the killers, who were mostly hired in Texas. As well as being well paid, each was insured for $3,000.

From a special train, 52 men, 22 of them from Texas, and most of them heavily armed, emerged at Casper, Wyoming. Two tame reporters were with the party; all wires had been cut; nearby Johnson County was isolated from the outside world.

Instead of heading directly for Buffalo, the invaders first went to deal with alleged rustlers at the KC Ranch. They arrived early on April 9th. It was a bitterly cold day with a hint of snow in the air, and in the hut were Nate Champion and Nick Ray, both on the death list. There were also two trappers staying overnight. They were the first to leave the hut and were caught and then released. When Ray opened the door to find out where they were, he was met with a hail of bullets and mortally wounded. Nate pulled him to safety as he crawled back.

There followed one of the West's greatest epics, for Nate kept up a day-long fight, even managing to write an account of it in a pocket book that was found later with a bullet through it and drenched in his blood. In one entry, written long after the battle had started, he confessed to feeling lonesome and wished he had a companion so that all sides could be watched at once. His enemies at last decided to burn him out and pushed a wagon, loaded with hay up to the cabin, then set it alight. His last entry was this:

Well, they have just got through shelling the house like hell. I heard them splitting wood. I guess they are going to fire the house tonight. I think I will make a break for it when night comes, if alive. It's not night yet. The house is all fired. Goodbye, boys, if I ever see you again.
NATHAN D. CHAMPION

He then ran through the back door of the cabin, Winchester in hand, pistol in his belt, bareheaded and in his stockings. 28 bullets tore into him, some hitting his brave heart. When his killers had glanced through his diary – erasing the name of Canton – they pinned a note to his vest which read: 'Cattle thieves, beware!'

Unbeknown to Nate, news had reached the outside after two passing men had observed what was happening and galloped away to Buffalo. The town erupted into action. Though Sheriff Angus was refused help from both the National Guard and the military, and though he found the wires cut and could not alert the governor – who would not have helped him – he soon raised a posse. Meanwhile, a member of the W.S.G.A. reached the invaders and urged them to turn back – 'The rustlers are massing from every direction!'

Having come a long way to fight, Canton and the Texans felt like doing just that, but the members of the Cheyenne Club were not so martially minded. They retreated to the TA Ranch and fortified it with a high barricade, trenches and earthworks. There they were besieged, the President being informed that Johnson County was in a state of armed insurrection. With the Texans and their employers falling out with each other, the Sixth Cavalry hastened to their rescue, three troops under Colonel Horn appearing just as the invaders thought they had finished their last breakfast.

Pompous Major Wolcott refused to surrender to Angus, but was prepared to be taken away in what amounted to protective custody by the military. The governor refused to have the invaders tried by a civilian court, and finally charges were dropped. The two trappers who could have given evidence were heavily bribed to get out of Wyoming. Frank Canton was later to boast that 'we had made it safe for an honest man to live in that county' – Johnson County – but he was a born liar. In the same autobiography he was to describe Dawson City as 'a picture of blood' in the peak year of the Klondike Stampede when, thanks to the Mounties, not a single man was murdered.

The gentlemen of the Cheyenne Club were never so powerful again, especially after their party, the Republicans, lost the election of 1892. Of course, there were doubtless a number of rustlers in Johnson County – who were less active from then onwards – but the cattle barons' case was destroyed by their methods. Those they had killed were remembered as martyrs, while Nate Champion, Texan that he was, was soon enshrined in Wyoming's – and the West's – Valhalla.

Guns and Gunfighters

Pistoleers / Gunfighters / Shootists/ Gunmen have appeared throughout this chapter, but it is now time to have a closer look at the exploits of a number of them, and at their weapons. All the descriptions above are authentically Western, though gunfighter is the most practical word. Joseph Rosa noted in the introduction to his *The Gunfighter: Man or Myth* that today the outlaw killer is commonly called a 'gunman' and the peace officer a 'gunfighter', but that he uses the latter term to cover both. So does this book. It was the alarming Clay Allison who promoted the word 'shootist' which was usually applied to experts – like himself.

Bat Masterson used the word 'man-killers' about the members of the fraternity to which he belonged. Today, when 'expert' fast-draw fans boast about their speed – not against a man-killer like John Wesley Hardin but against the clock – it is worth looking more closely at the methods and motivation of Masterson; how he and his like took their time and placed their shots and were prepared to kill and maim. Naturally, speed mattered, but accuracy mattered more, or, as the old Frontier statement put it: 'Speed's fine, but accuracy's final.' As for fanning the pistol – slapping the hammer to recock, the index finger of the other hand holding the trigger pressed – this 'technique', so beloved by Hollywood directors down the years, was inevitably so innaccurate that it was only useful for firing into a crowd. In Masterson's opinion, based on considerable experience, the gunfighter needed proficiency in the use of firearms and deliberation.

The 'Equalizer'

The old Frontier saying, 'God created man, but it was Sam Colt's revolver that made him equal', was fair comment. With an 'equalizer' in his hand, and assuming that he knew how to handle it, a weakling could stand up to a stronger man and win.

The chances were that the pistol (as revolvers were usually called in the West) would be a Colt, named for the great Samuel Colt (1814–62). Colt did not invent the revolver, but he was the first to produce a practical and reliable version, patenting his design in England in 1835 and in his native America the following year, the first weapons being five-shot. They were used against the Seminole Indians in Florida in the late 1830s, and in the early 1840s the Texas Rangers startled the Comanches, the 'Lords of the South Plains', with the deadly new weapons.

These were percussion weapons, meaning that they were loaded with cap and ball, and their charge was set off by a small copper cap which contained fulminate of mercury. This was put on a nipple or small tube at the back of the chamber. It was detonated when the hammer hit it.

In 1846, the Colt Walker made its appearance, named for ex-Ranger Sam Walker. It was a big .44 calibre six-shooter that could propel a ball more than 600 yards (550 m), its original muzzle velocity being 1,500 feet (457 m) per second. In 1848, the 'Dragoon' or 'Army' appeared, but it was the Colt's Navy revolver of 1851 that became the weapon of the gunfighters.

The Navy was a close-range weapon except when handled by an expert shot, 'close-range' meaning up to 25 yards (23 m). The Colt New Model Army was introduced in 1860, by which time there were also a number of pocket pistols available. Then in 1873 came the most celebrated pistol of them all.

This was the Colt Single Action Army revolver, model of 1873, a .45 calibre masterpiece known as the Peacemaker. Except for a break from 1941 to 1955, it has been in production ever since. It still uses a mechanism that dates back to 1847!

Like its rivals – among whom were Smith and Wesson and Remington – the .45 had 'fixed' or metallic ammunition. Its cap, ball and powder were contained in a copper or brass case. Not all gunfighters made the Peacemaker their first choice, some preferring the Smith and Wesson .44 'American' revolver.

The Winchester, model of 1873, was undoubtedly the most famous rifle of the Wild West period; indeed it became so popular that Colt's rechambered a number of .45s in 1878 to take its cartridge. Each was called a 'Frontier Six-Shooter'.

Some Shootists

Only a handful of gunfighters rank as Frontier immortals, men like Hickok, Billy the Kid, Jesse James and Wyatt Earp who are known by name even by millions with little interest in the West.

Before any of them sprang to fame a notorious badman named Jack Slade (1824–64) had the good fortune to be profiled by the young Mark Twain, who wrote about him in *Roughing It*:

Slade was a matchless marksman with a navy revolver. The legends say that one morning at Rocky Ridge, when he was feeling comfortable, he saw a man approaching who had offended him some days before – observe the fine memory he had for matters like that – and, 'Gentlemen,' said Slade, drawing, 'it is a good twenty-five yard shot – I'll clip the third button on his coat!' Which he did. The bystanders all admired it. And they all attended the funeral too.

Slade, having fought in the Mexican War (1846–48) and spent some time in Kansas, joined the Central Overland California and Pike's Peak Express Company, rising to be a line superintendent. He was sent to Julesburg by his boss to check whether Jules Bene, also a superintendent, was horse-stealing as well as being a member of a gang of outlaws. The pair were soon facing each other in town and Jules, who was a French-Canadian, pumped three bullets into Slade before he could draw. Next, both barrels of Bene's shotgun were emptied into Slade and Jules ordered him to be buried. Instead, the spectators started to string Bene up and only the arrival of their overall boss, Ben Ficklin saved him. Slade was still breathing and Bene was told to leave the area or else.

Left: Jack Slade using the unfortunate Jules Bene for target practice.

Right: W. R. Leigh's picture of a fleeing bandit (who is wielding a Colt single action .45 of 1873).

Unwisely, Bene returned and Slade's loyal boys tied him to a corral post and sent word to their boss – who arrived and starting filling Bene with lead in between drinks. Finally, feeling rather tired, Slade forced the barrel of his gun into Bene's mouth and pulled the trigger. Not yet satisfied, he then cut Bene's ears off and, so legend has it, used one of them – suitably pickled – as a fob for his watch, and the other to pay for a round of drinks.

It was drink that was the death of him, for while ranching in Montana, he drank so much and became so rowdy that no one could stand him. Vigilantes hanged him as his unfortunate wife screamed abuse at them.

Clay Allison

Robert A. Clay Allison was known as a bad man to fool with. Born in Tennessee in 1840, he joined up for the Civil War despite a club foot. A doctor diagnosed him as 'partly epileptic and partly maniacal'. He knew his job.

He went with his family to Texas after the war and became a rancher and dedicated drinker. After leading a lynch mob against a killer – one of whose victims was Clay's daughter – he cut off his head and stuck it in the local saloon on a pole. He gradually became more and more eccentric, taking on a man called Bowman in a saloon, both men being drunk and down to their underwear, and both shooting at the other's feet to find out who danced best under fire. Neither was injured!

Killings and lynchings continued, one man being 'executed' after eating with Clay, the latter not wanting to send a man to hell on an empty stomach. On another occasion he shot his club foot, and on yet another he and an enemy arranged to fight in a grave with Bowie knives – and with both men stark naked.

Even his death was off-beat, for when bringing back supplies to his ranch by wagon, he tried to stop a sack of grain from falling to the ground, fell himself, and was fatally wounded when one of the wagon wheels went over his neck. This prevented the naked duel in the grave from taking place.

Another epic event which may or

Tennessee-born Clay Allison's life reads like a horror comic.

Bill Longley killed 32 men. There were few friends at his hanging.

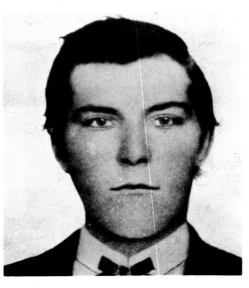

John Wesley Hardin, a preacher's son, with an un-Christian aptitude for killing.

may not have happened concerned a visit by him to a dentist in Cheyenne. He complained to the dentist that he had toothache and the wretched man started working on the wrong tooth. Furious, Clay left his seat, found another, more efficient operative, then returned to the first dentist and took out one of his teeth. Starting on a second tooth he was only restrained when the dentist's screams caused people to rush to his assistance.

Bill Longley

William P. Longley (1851–78) was a grim Texan in a bitter period of his state's history. Even law-abiding folk felt not just the bitterness of defeat but anger at the hated state police, most of them chosen by the conquerors because they were ex-slaves. Longley would have no doubt been a badman in any period but the poisonous atmosphere in Reconstruction Texas made him even worse. He and the press claimed he had killed 32 men, most of them Blacks. That was during his trial in 1877 which led to his execution. Four thousand were there to see him hanged, and his words as he waited for the drop were memorable: 'I see a good many enemies around and mighty few friends.' His death was horrible, for his feet touched the ground on the first drop and he was pulled up and hanged once more, taking eleven minutes to die.

John Wesley Hardin

Longley was jealous of Hardin (1853–95), resenting the younger man's fame. Famous he was, for when the law caught up with him in 1878, he boasted that he had killed 44 men, and there is no reason to believe that he was lying. Like Longley, he was a badman made worse by Reconstruction Texas, and like him he was a hardened killer. When he went up the Abilene Trail in 1871 as a cowboy, he had already killed 12 men and this was to reach 20 in Kansas. In Abilene he shot a man through the wall of his hotel room. The unfortunate victim in the next room was guilty of the crime of snoring, disturbing Hardin's reading of a newspaper.

Marshall Wild Bill Hickok was

furious when he heard the news, not least because he and the younger gunfighter had been on friendly terms and Hardin had behaved himself in town. The marshal was too late. Hardin escaped in his undershirt.

It was the Rangers who finally caught him, cornering him in a train in Florida in 1877. He was not released from prison until 1894, by which time his much-loved wife had died. Having studied law in prison, he tried his luck in El Paso, but loss of morale and too much drink did his new career no good. In 1895, local lawman, John Selman, murdered him, shooting him in the back in the Acme Saloon. Hardin's famous autobiography is probably authentic and definitely worth reading.

Sam Bass

Sam Bass (1851–78) was lucky to have a very good song written about him, beginning with the line, 'Sam Bass was born in Indiana', and complete with a catchy tune. So, despite a not very notable career as a badman, his memory lives on.

Taking to crime for excitement, though horse-racing was his particular love, he and some friends, robbed a Union Pacific train in Nebraska. Subsequently, he formed his own gang in Texas and realised some success. He acquired a kind of Robin Hood reputation and certainly, unlike most badmen, gave away some money — not, of course, his own. Finally, the Rangers found him at Round Rock in 1878, helped by one of his own gang who turned traitor. He died on his 27th birthday.

The Downfall of Dallas Stoudenmire

He was as fine a looking lawman as any law-abiding citizens could hope to see patrolling their streets, but Marshal Stoudenmire (1845–82), the man who had tamed El Paso, Texas, had two problems. One was a feud with El Paso's leading racketeers, the Manning Brothers, the other was drink. Once a Texas Ranger, Stoudenmire, who had survived many wounds fighting for the Confederates, was fired from his El Paso job because

of his drinking habits.

On September 18th, 1882, he and another ex-policeman, Walt Jones, headed for the Coliseum Saloon to confront the Mannings. 'Doc' Manning was playing billiards and Jim was by the bar – until he saw the enemy and went to get his brother Frank. Laying down his cue, 'Doc' started arguing with Stoudenmire.

Gunsmoke was the inevitable result, the ex-marshal pushing away his friend as he and 'Doc' went for their pistols.

His friend's action lost Stoudenmire invaluable time, Manning getting off the first shot with his double-action .44. Fortunately, the ball lodged in a pocket book and some letters in Stoudenmire's right breast pocket, but Manning swiftly fired again into Dallas' left breast. Staggering back, he managed to fire, hitting 'Doc' above his right elbow. Dropping his gun, Manning hurled himself at his enemy and, despite his wound, hugged the ex-marshal to him, preventing him from firing again.

A nightmare dance followed which led the short racketeer and the tall Stoudenmire right out into the street – at which moment Jim Manning reappeared brandishing a .45. So highly strung were his nerves that his first shot hit a barber's pole, but his second shot was more controlled and Dallas was hit in the head and died.

The nightmare achieved an extra dimension now, for when 'Doc' had pulled himself free, he grabbed one of his victim's guns and began battering the dead man's head with it until bystanders pulled him away. Both Mannings were tried and freed. The death of Stoudenmire, the once great lawman with a drink problem, proved

Top left: The silver star of a Marshal of Abilene, Kansas.

Top right: The badge of a U.S. Deputy Marshal, Oklahoma Territory, c.1895.

Above: Texas Ranger badge.

155

156

yet again that a gunfighter's faculties had to be kept intact if he was to have a chance of long term survival.

Lucky Luke Short

Luke Short (1854–93) was a gambler and saloon owner with good friends on the police force of Dodge City during its heyday as a cowtown. He was also a skilled gunfighter, though he was lucky the day he met Jim Courtright, the long-haired marshal of Fort Worth on February 8th, 1887.

Short had moved to Texas after some trouble with the city authorities in Dodge and now in Forth Worth he had two problems, a protection racket and Courtright. On February 8th, word reached Short that the lawman wanted him. He left his place of work, the White Elephant Saloon, and, as requested, met Courtright on the street.

The dapper gambler faced the marshal tucking his thumbs into the armholes of his waistcoat. When he began lowering them, appearing to be smoothing out his waistcoat, the marshal warned him not to go for his gun. 'I'm not trying to pull a gun,' said the aggrieved Short. 'I haven't got a gun there, see!' As if to show his innocence, he pulled at his coat.

Taking no chances, Courtright drew his gun and so did Luke, who fired wildly. The story goes that the bullet hit the marshal's thumb as he drew and cocked his pistol. Desperately, he tried to shift his weapon to his left hand, but Short killed him with three shots. That is the Texas legend, but Courtright's pistol told a different story. The cylinder was jammed and could not have turned. The attempted use of the 'Border shift' as it is known, makes a better story, but seems not to have been true. As for Luke Short, he died young in 1893 – of dropsy.

Showdown at Holbrook

Only one Western gunfight deserves to be called astounding. It took place on September 4th, 1887 in Holbrook,

Left: Black Jack Ketchum's head was torn from his body when he finally paid for his crimes in 1901.

Arizona during the ferocious Pleasant Valley War (see page 142), but it was not a part of it even though Andy Blevins, who called himself Andy Cooper because of a murder he had committed in Texas, had been taking part in it on the Graham side. When he hit town that September day he started boasting in a saloon how he had killed a Tewksbury supporter just two days earlier, after which he headed for home.

Into Holbrook that afternoon rode Apache County's new sheriff, the oddly named Commodore Perry Owens. His father had been an admirer of the naval hero, Commodore Perry. The citizens of Holbrook were not impressed by what they saw, for decorating the sheriff's pleasant face was long hair that was by now outdated as a fashion. Again, his Colt butt was forward and his chaps decorative to say the least, both outdated fashions also.

In fact, Owen was a product of cattle drives and a dead shot. He was tracking down Blevins for stealing horses from the Navaho. He was warmly welcomed at home by his mother, brother Johnny and his kid brother Houston. The house was packed that day, for also there were his brother-in-law, Mose Roberts, Johnny Blevins' wife, a Mrs. Gladden and her young daughter.

Both Johnny and Andy had seen Owens ride into town and got home fast. Owens cleaned his pistol, then, being tipped off that Andy would soon leave town, walked towards the Blevins house, Winchester in hand. The house stood 15 feet from the street and Owens saw Andy saddling a horse; he spotted the sheriff as well however, and darted indoors.

Owens, walking up the steps to the porch, saw Andy and three others staring at him through the window and ordered his quarry out. Andy carefully opened the door using his left hand, his pistol in his right, then Johnny came through the side door off the porch and Owens was between the brothers. The sheriff stared steadily at Owens, whose nerves presumably stopped him from acting.

'Cooper!' said the sheriff, 'I want you!'

'What do you want with me?' asked

Andy, to be told that the lawman had a warrant for him. Playing for time, he asked for more details and if he could see about the matter, but Owens wanted him now.

The St. John's *Herald* of September 8th, 1887 reported what happened next, as did the proceedings of the inquest, where Mrs. Blevins and her daughter-in-law hopefully informed the court that Andy was unarmed!

Andy refused to go and both men fired, Andy falling back with a wound that would prove mortal. Owens was not hit. Johnny Blevins, meanwhile, had fired and missed, but hit Andy's horse. Owens now swung round, fired, and sent a bullet into Johnny's shoulder.

Mrs. Blevins took the dying Andy into the house, while Owens retired to the street to cover the house more completely. When he saw Andy at a window, he fired at him.

Mose Roberts suddenly erupted through a window or a door in the corner of the building, pistol in hand, but before he could fire, Owens had thrown himself to one side of a wagon and fired, mortally wounding Roberts. He managed to stagger to the comparative safety of the house, where Sam Houston Blevins, aged 16, and still without a criminal record, was bent on revenge. The wounded Johnny would not give up his gun, so he seized the dying Andy's and, as his desperate mother tried to restrain him, he tore out of the front door. The deadly Winchester spoke again and the youth fell back dead into his mother's arms.

And now there was silence, broken only by weeping and the groans of the wounded. Commodore Perry Owens turned his back on the house and walked away. His epic battle had lasted less than a minute.

After three years as sheriff, Owens, who later cut his hair, became a railroad detective, a Wells Fargo Messenger and, lastly, a businessman, dying in his sixties in 1918.

Gunfight at the OK Corral

The most famous of the Earp clan was born in Illinois in 1848 and died in 1929, aged 80. For a notorious gunfighter to live to such an age was

not the least of Wyatt Earp's achievements. His great fame, however, is due to his biographer Stuart Lake, who created an Earp who was a veritable St. George of the West, whereas his only true claim to Western immortality is his much argued-over period in Tombstone, Arizona.

His career as a lawman began in Wichita in 1875, before which he had been, amongst other things, a buffalo hunter and a horse thief. At Wichita he was an efficient officer, but was dismissed for fighting, moving on to Dodge City where he served periods as assistant marshal until 1879. Again, his efficiency was noted and – like most good con men – he looked good, adding to his credit by religious observances.

After being run out of Mobeetie, Texas, for swindling in 1879, he and some of his family, plus his gunfighting dentist friend, Doc Holliday, gathered in Las Vegas, New Mexico. The next stop was Tombstone, Arizona.

Assembled there were Wyatt's elder brother Virgil, as well as James and Morgan Earp and assorted wives and mistresses. James, wounded in the Civil War, was to take no part in the very different warfare in Tombstone that has been controversial ever since.

Tombstone had been named by Ed Schieffelin, who struck silver in the area in 1878. He had been looking for stones, meaning quartz, and a friend had warned him – for this was Apache country – 'the only stone you are gonna find'll be your tombstone'.

Doc Holliday joined the Earps and in October 1880; brother Virgil became city marshal when Fred White was killed. Virgil had been his deputy.

"ED" SCHIEFFELIN.

Wyatt was established at the Oriental Saloon, having an interest in it, also at the Eagle Brewery, where he ran the faro table. He became deputy sheriff of Pima County.

Tension was now building up between the ranchers and cowboys on one hand and the mining interests on the other. The Earps, were officially neutral, but, being Northerners, had no liking for the cowboy element and fell out with the Clanton and McClaury families, who were said to rustle as well as raise cattle, and no doubt did.

The climax was long in coming and much detail must be omitted. The cowboy faction had a supporter in Johnny Behan, newly-elected sheriff of the recently formed Cochise County, whose votes he needed. He soon fell out with the Earps, arresting Doc Holliday on the reasonable suspicion that he had killed a stage driver during a robbery. Rumour had it that the Earps had planned the robbery.

Relations worsened. Virgil, as a deputy U.S. Marshal, arrested two of Behan's men for stage robbery, Frank McClaury challenged Morgan Earp to a duel, then, on October 25th, 1881, Doc Holliday called the unarmed Ike Clanton a 'damn son of a cowboy'. The insult was hurled over a lunch counter and Ike endured shouts of 'Go get heeled' as he left. At that moment Wyatt and Virgil appeared. Morgan was watching the confrontation and, as Ike ran off, he implored Morgan not to shoot him in the back.

After a night of drinking and poker, Ike felt better and appeared on the street with a rifle and pistol, only to be forced to his knees by a blow on his head from the barrel of Virgil's pistol.

He was then arrested for carrying firearms in town and fined. As the next victim was Tom McClaury, pistol-whipped to the ground by Wyatt, rivalry between the factions reached new and venomous proportions. Only Doc Holliday was minding his own business playing poker through the night.

On the morning of the 26th, the Earps heard that Ike and Billy Clanton, Tom and Frank McClaury, and Billy Claiborne, were at the OK Corral. Wyatt and Morgan started towards it, being joined by Doc Holliday, carrying a shotgun. Johnny Behan asked Virgil not to fight his enemies but to disarm them, but was brushed aside. He found Doc and Morgan, but Virgil now appeared with a shotgun. Trying to do his duty, the wretched Behan now came upon Frank McClaury who was holding a horse – and who also refused to surrender his guns. However, he walked with Behan to Fly's Photographic Gallery.

Outside the gallery, whose owner has left us so many historic photographs of old Arizona, were the Clantons, Tom McClaury and Billy Claiborne. Ike and Tom were unarmed; Billy Clanton and Billy Claiborne were armed but refused to part with them unless the enemy did so too. Behan urged the quartet to accompany him to his office, at which moment the Earps and Doc Holliday came into view in a lethal-looking line. When Behan tried to halt them, he was pushed away by Virgil. He had made his brothers and Doc deputies for the occasion.

The gunfight did not in fact take place in the corral, but in Fremont Street in front of Fly's establishment. It was a close range affair, with the Earps some six to eight feet from the Clantons, who were in line with a private house at the back of them.

Behan had had enough and fled behind Fly's house, to be joined by Claiborne. According to Behan, Wyatt now shouted: 'You sons of bitches, you have been looking for a fight and now you have it.' Wyatt Earp's very different version had Virgil ordering the opposition to give up their arms at which Frank McClaury and Billy Clanton dropped their hands to their guns. Then Virgil, said Wyatt, called: 'Hold, I don't mean that. I've come to disarm you!' Considering the events of the past 24 hours, his alleged words seem a trifle tame.

'Don't shoot me, I don't want to fight,' called Billy Clanton, and Tom McClaury opened his coat to prove he was unarmed. Then the fight started.

Wyatt and Billy may have shot first, the former hitting Frank McClaury in the stomach. He only got off one shot before he lurched away. Billy had shot and missed Wyatt and now the gunfight began in earnest. Ike raced up to Wyatt and grabbed his arm, at which Wyatt told him to fight or get away. He ran for cover – safely, despite a blast from Holliday's shotgun.

Tom McLaury had tried to get Frank's Winchester from his saddle scabbard and then use the horse for cover. Billy Clanton was wounded twice by Morgan, first in the right arm, then in the chest. He leant back against Fly's place desperately trying to get his pistol into action. Tom died when Frank's horse reared and exposed him, Doc blasting him with his shotgun. The badly wounded Billy managed to wound Virgil in the calf, and he fell to the ground, while the dying Frank exchanged shots with Doc until Morgan killed him. Holliday's luck was in for he had his hip skinned and his holster was sent flying.

Brave Billy Clanton's last shot hit Morgan in the shoulder. As he fell, he shot Billy; so did Wyatt and the youth lay dying.

There was a moment's silence, then Fly ran from his house and disarmed Billy. 'Give me some more cartridges' were his last words. There were three men dead and three more badly wounded in a fight that had lasted less than a minute. The only two men to emerge unscathed were Wyatt Earp and Ike Clanton.

Tensions ran high in town, but a 30-day hearing cleared the Earps of blame even though the judge had doubts about Virgil's choice of deputies. The winners had many enemies still, and Virgil was crippled for life when a shotgun blasted his side two months after the fight, fired by an unknown avenger. He lived on until 1905. In March 1882, another Earp was hit, this time fatally, Morgan being killed playing pool. Again, the avenger was unknown. Wyatt believed that the chief culprits were Frank Stilwell and Pete Spence and later killed the former when he found him beside the train that was to take Morgan's body back to the Earp's family home in California. It was claimed that Stilwell had tried to kill Wyatt. Whatever the truth, he was speedily lying beside the tracks with six bullets in him. Spence wisely gave himself up to the authorities, but the Earps found another victim, a half-blood named Florentino Cruz, executed at Spence's wood camp. Then the surviving Earps left the state. One day, perhaps, someone will produce an authoritative biography of Wyatt Earp that will solve the enigma of his character. Until then, his friends and enemies will continue to fight over his memory.

Left: Doc Holliday, the 'gunfighting dentist' who died of tuberculosis in 1887.

Top right: Playing Faro at Morenci, Arizona Territory, 1895.

Right: The aftermath of the Gunfight at the OK Corral. L. to R. Tom and Frank McLaury and Billy Claiborne.

REMAINS OF McLAURY-EARP
TOMBSTONE, ARIZONA

CHAPTER ELEVEN
TRANSPORTATION WEST

Transportation is a sober word to use about the saga of Western steamboats, stagecoaches and railroads. As for the Pony Express, even cynical Mark Twain, as we shall see, was reduced to rapture at the sight of one of its young riders galloping along. Western transportation, in fact, unlike so much of the story of the real West, was truly romantic in many respects. In others it was a mixture of know-how, endurance and sweat.

Steamboats arrived first. For 60 years or so, they were the monarchs of the Mississippi, Missouri and other Western rivers. They ranged from veritable floating palaces to what were virtual gunboats, armoured and ready for action against 'hostiles' on the upper reaches of the Missouri. Large or small, nearly all looked impressive, as smoke rose from their long funnels and paddles flashed in the sun.

Their importance was never in doubt. Businessmen, ordinary passengers and Westerners along the rivers depended on them for a multitude of uses, from transporting cotton and other goods to bringing back the wounded from Indian fights.

The steamboat age opened on the Mississipi when the *New Orleans* started trading between Natchez, Mississipi, and New Orleans in 1811. Just seven years later, a steamboat puffed slowly up part of the Missouri.

Left: 'Maxwell House'.

Opposite page: A Mississippi River steamboat of the 1880s.

The 1840s were the golden age of the steamboats, a steady decline starting in the 1870s because of railroads. Though there are large barges on the rivers still, the only mementoes of earlier days are some splendid tourist vessels.

In the great days steamboat captains were kings on water. Most of them owned their own boats, and many spent fortunes on furnishing them in grand style. There was no financial risk in this, for costs could be recovered in a single season.

'Captains' is hardly an adequate word for these magnificoes, for as well as being very skilled rivermen, they had to be bankers and merchants, and totally trustworthy. A plantation owner would hand over his whole stock of cotton or sugar to a captain, who would later sell it for him at the highest market price. Farmers and ranchers trusted them as well.

It was business on an enormous scale. By 1846, for instance, there were 1,190 steamboats on Western rivers, carrying some $400 million worth of freight, while by the 1860s, the lower Missouri was even more busy than the Mississippi. Mark Twain called the Mississippi the crookedest river in the world, having been a pilot's apprentice in his youth. He set his two most famous books, *Tom Sawyer* and *Huckleberry Finn*, beside and on her.

In fact, the pilots of the river were almost as important as the captains, as a classic yarn illustrates. Three hopefuls applied for the job of pilot, two of them telling the captain that they had never hit a snag nor run aground in 20 years on the river.

The third would-be pilot said: 'Cap'n, I know this river better than any livin' man. I guess there ain't a mudbank or sandbar that I ain't hit in my time.'

The captain grasped the applicant's hand. 'You're my man,' he said warmly. 'You really know the river!'

Though many steamboats were wood-burners, many more burnt coal. Both were liable to blow up. A passenger gave novelist Charles Dickens good advice on the subject in 1842. 'They generally blow up forward,' he told him, so it is not surprising that the best accommodation was at the stern.

Because many Western rivers were shallow, steamboats were built to suit them. Instead of the magnificent floating palaces that were typical of the Mississippi steamboats, the Missouri River sternwheeler was designed, the wheel descending only a few inches into the stream. Amazingly, such a boat could carry 30 cabin passengers and 200 tons of freight through waist-high water. This meant that steamboats could reach far up rivers all over the West.

Occasionally, a major figure appeared who controlled an empire as big as a cattle king's. Such a tycoon was Henry Villard, who bought up the Oregon Steam Navigation Company for $5 million in 1879, while he was busy promoting the Northern Pacific Railway. The next decade saw him the owner of a vast rail and steamboat company.

For relaxation – to say nothing of publicity – steamboat kings liked promoting a good race, though these greatly increased the chances of an explosion. The most celebrated of all river races was that between the *Natchez* and the *Robert E. Lee* in 1870. The course was from New Orleans to St. Louis and millions of Southerners rejoiced when the *Lee* won because she was named after the South's beloved military commander in the recent Civil War.

Yet for all the fame of Captain Cannon of the *Lee* and Captain Leathers of the *Natchez*, their duel was a minor exploit compared with the feat of the little known Captain Grant Marsh of the *Far West*.

On June 27th, 1876, a Crow Indian boarded the ship at the mouth of the Little Bighorn in Montana and told him how Custer and his command had been wiped out. Soon General Terry appeared to order him to be ready to rush 52 wounded men from the rest of the 7th down river – 710 miles down the Bighorn, the wild, uncharted Yellowstone, then the Missouri, to Fort Lincoln.

That nightmare journey through turbulent waters, with one stop to ferry troops across river and a second one for supplies, lasted from the evening of July 3rd to 11 pm on July 5th, an average of almost 350 miles a

Above: The race between The Natchez *and the* Robert E. Lee.

Left: The Little Eagle *on the Missouri near Leavenworth, Kansas.*

166

day. Grant Marsh's speed record was never beaten, and, more important, 51 of the wounded survived in what truly ranks as the greatest steamboat race of them all.

The muted finale of Western steamboats came with the Klondike stampede of 1898, when, for a year or two, some were to be seen sailing up and down the Yukon and its tributaries.

The glory days had gone for ever.

The Pony Express

It was wildly expensive to run, and out-of-date the year after it started. It helped bring about the downfall of its creators, Russell, Majors and Waddell. Yet the Pony Express, world-famous while it was operating,

has never been forgotten and remains one of the supreme stories of the American West.

Gold Rush California badly needed a first-rate mail service to link it with the East. As we shall see, John Butterfield started an overland mail route in 1857, but its big swing to the south – thanks to pressure by Southern politicians – resulted in a journey

from St. Louis to California of 22–24 days.

This was not good enough for Californians, and William Russell, an official of the Central Overland California and Pike's Peak Express Company, founded the subsidiary firm of Russell, Majors and Waddell with Alexander Majors and William Waddell. The C.O.C. & P.P.E. had acquired the nickname 'Clean Outa Cash & Past Paying Expenses' line. Russell and his friends were to be out of cash, but no-one in his senses would have sneered at the feat of organization that they achieved.

Along what was roughly the old Oregon–California Trail were built 190 stations staffed by 400 stationmen. Twenty-five of the stations were for changes of riders and called 'home' stations, the rest were for changes of mounts, and were known as 'swing' stations. Some 500 fast, wiry horses were bought and 80 riders were hired, 40 more being taken on later. Their average age was 18, they had to be

Preceding pages: The Pony Express – The first rider leaving St Joseph, Missouri, on 3 April 1860.

Above: A Pony Express saddle with a mochila over it – a knapsack with pouches for mail. The mochila was transferred from horse to horse at high speed.

Right: A Pony Express station with a rider coming in for a new mount.

light, but strong and with powers of endurance. They were sworn to be sober, decent in speech and gentlemanly in conduct. That they had to be very brave goes without saying. The famous advertisement was clear about that: 'Wanted – young, skinny, wiry fellows, not over 18. Must be expert riders, willing to risk death daily. Orphans preferred. Wages $25 a week.'

Seventy-five horses would be used

Above: A Pony Express rider pursued by Indians.

Left: A weary-looking group of young Pony Express riders.

in each direction for a run. At each relay station, the boy rider would have two minutes to throw his saddlebags on to his next mount and race away again. And after riding a set distance, one rider would hand over his mail to the next. Though the service later became twice weekly, it started as a weekly service.

The riders had to behave themselves. Swearing and drinking were forbidden and each was given a Bible – also a revolver and a rifle, though these were for self defence. They wore red shirts and blue trousers.

Saddles were lightweight, and mail was strictly limited to letters and telegrams. The letters had to be written on thin paper and protected in oilcloth from the weather.

The amazing trio set up their Pony Express in a mere 60 days. 'The Greatest Enterprise of Modern Times', as the firm's publicity proudly proclaimed, started operating from St. Joseph, Missouri, and from San Francisco on April 3rd, 1860. Sacramento was reached in only ten days, and when horse and rider completed their journey to San Francisco by boat, there was a grand parade awaiting them. Two thousand miles away in Missouri there were also celebrations. The Pony Express was spectacularly in business.

The young riders usually survived hazards that included Indians, raging rivers, blizzards and wild animals, but a boy's luck could run out. One arrived at a station in Nevada slumped dead over his saddle, his body riddled with arrows. He was clutching the mane of his horse so tightly that a station hand had to cut it from his grasp. The mail was safe.

Riders covered from 35–75 miles before passing the mail on, depending on the terrain. They were expected to average nine mph, though on good terrain, thirty might be achieved.

There were some amazing feats. 'Pony Bob' Haslam, finding himself in the middle of a war with the Paiutes, ranged backwards and forwards with mail, covering 380 miles in 36 hours riding, with one break of eight hours sleep. He returned to his normal duties, the richer by $100 donated by his grateful bosses.

The worst disasters normally occurred at stations, for the riders' ponies could usually outstrip Indian pursuers, Indian horses not having such good feed as those of the Pony Express. Nick Wilson, who had lived with Shoshoni before his Pony Express days, was once pursued by a band of 13 Indians. His horse had 'grain-fed muscles', as he later put it, muscles that saved him from Indian arrows and bullets. His pursuers' horses were grass-fed.

Bill Campbell, who was never to forget how he carried Abraham Lincoln's first innaugural address in his saddlebag, was once pursued by timber wolves, who rapidly caught up with him. He killed two of them with his pistol, and the pack stopped to devour their former friends.

Equipment was modified to lighten the overall load, the rifle being abandoned, plus one of the two pistols the first riders carried, for it was speed that mattered most to the riders. As for the record run, young William Cody, long before he was Buffalo Bill, achieved a continuous ride of 384 miles – or did he? He did not start claiming it until his days as a showman. It is hard not to award the palm to Pony Bob Haslam, for, apart from the feat noted above, his exploits included a 120-mile run which ended with a bullet-shattered arm and a jaw smashed by an arrow. No wonder it was not just along the trail that the Pony Express boys were so admired. News of their feats was sent East by reporters stationed in St. Louis, and soon they were being talked about far beyond America.

Mark Twain was one of the lucky ones who actually saw a rider in action. It was in Nevada, and in *Roughing It*, he described the moment:

Away across the endless dead level of the prairie a black speck appears against the sky, and it is plain that it moves. Well, I should think so! In a second or two it becomes a horse and rider, rising and falling – sweeping toward us nearer and nearer – growing more and more distinct, more and more sharply defined – nearer and still nearer, and the flutter of the hoofs comes faintly to the ear – another instant a whoop and a hurrah from our upper deck, a wave of the rider's hand, but no reply, and man and horse burst past our excited faces and go swinging away like a belated fragment of a storm!

Suddenly it was all over. In 1861, the transcontinental telegraph was completed. Russell and his partners were deeply in debt, for their spectacular operation had cost far more to set up and maintain than they could ever recover in fees. They had had no government subsidy, and though nearly 35,000 items of mail had been carried, the fees charged nowhere near paid for the mammoth organization that had been so swiftly built up.

Yet despite the crash, which saw the trio forced to sell their stage operation to Ben Holladay, the 'King of Hurry', whom we shall soon be meeting, the Pony Express influenced the future of the West. Firstly, the young riders proved a sensational advertisement for the West, and, secondly, the riders showed that even on horseback a central route across the Plains and mountains was practical. By the end of the decade, a railroad followed.

Stagecoaching Days

Romantic as stagecoach travel tends to look in Westerns, only the unimaginative fail to grasp that it was an uncomfortable business at best. The *Omaha Herald* of October 3rd, 1877, gave travellers some tips:

In very cold weather abstain entirely from liquor when on the road; because you will freeze twice as quickly when under its influence. Don't growl at the food received at the station; stage companies generally provide the best they can get.

Don't keep the stage waiting. Don't smoke a strong pipe inside the coach – spit on the leeward side. If you have anything to drink in a bottle pass it around. Procure your stimulants before starting as 'ranch' (Stage Depot) whiskey is not 'nectar'.

Don't swear or lop over neighbours when sleeping. Take small change to pay expenses. Never shoot on the road as the noise might frighten the horses. Don't discuss politics or religion. Don't point out where murders have been committed especially if there are women passengers.

And so on . . .

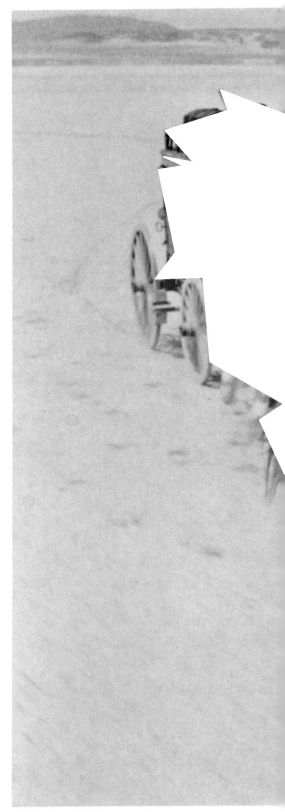

Above: A Wells Fargo Concord Coach.

174

A final warning was a masterpiece of understatement. 'Expect annoyances, discomfort, and some hardship.'

The Californian Gold Rush hastened the coming of transcontinental road and rail travel. The East recognized the need to bring the Far West under its control. Californians knew that roads would bring prices down in the mining camps and desperately wanted news. Such was the pressure that subsidies were regularly granted from the mid-fifties to the early 1870s to help stage lines and railroads. Extra pressure was exerted by Southern politicians to make the most of Southern routes, for the 1850s saw the steady march towards seccession and civil war. This was why Butterfield, mentioned earlier, pioneered the much longer southern route, for the postmaster general, Aaron V. Brown of Tennessee, being a dedicated Southerner, threw out the bids of Northern companies. These had naturally championed a route similar to the Oregon–California Trail.

It took the Butterfield Overland Express a year to get organized. Along the 2,800 miles from Tipton, Missouri, to San Francisco wood or 'adobe' stations were erected at 10-

mile intervals, each run by an agent characterized by Ray Billington in his great *Westerly Expansion* as being 'usually a profane cut-throat wanted by half a dozen vigilance committees, and every 200 miles of road was entrusted to a "district agent" who differed from his unruly subordinates only in being quicker on the draw'.

One thousand or so mules were hired by the company, 500 horses, and also drivers, most of them, according to Billington, swaggering bullies. We may be sure that Bibles were not issued to them.

Butterfield proved he could cover his route in just under 25 days at an average of 5 mph, horses being changed every 10 miles. Passengers paid $200 for the trip, but were less important than the mails. Two types of vehicle were used, the light Celerity wagon and, more notably, the great Concord coach.

Developed by the Abbot-Downing Company of Concord, New Hampshire, this proved better than any other coach for the deserts and plains of the West. It was strong and comfortable, the carriage being suspended on two thorough-braces – shock absorbers of thick strips of leather. The heavy wheels, with their iron tires that prevented sinking into soft sand, were wide enough to prevent the coach from tipping over. Nine could be packed inside, while above them were seated the driver and conductor. Wells

Fargo coaches had an express messenger beside the driver riding shotgun. In all, up to 22 could be packed aboard, with 12 on top.

Professionals greatly admired the Concord. One said: 'It don't break down: it only wears out.' This was disputed by those who claimed that it never wore out. One was under water for a month, was recovered, and served another half century!

The Butterfield operation started on September 15th, 1858, from San Francisco and Tipton. Two set out in each direction every week. The mail made the money, for usually there were not many passengers due to the

price and the rugged length of the trip. Apache and Comanche sometimes attacked stations and also coaches. One driver gave up his job, explaining to Mark Twain that he left the Butterfield route as 'he came as near to starving to death in the midst of abundance, because they kept him so leaky with bullet holes that he couldn't hold his vittels'. It was Mark Twain who, not minding the rocking motion of the Concord, called it 'a cradle on wheels'.

By 1858, Russell, Majors and Waddell had built up freighting empire on the central plains, using 3,500 covered wagons, 4,000 men and

Left: Freight Wagon.

Below: Union Pacific track layers at work in Nebraska in 1867.

40,000 draft oxen. Wagon trains headed westwards: 25 covered wagons, each with three tons of goods, and each hauled by 12 oxen, who were in the charge of a 'bullwhacker', complete with a 12-foot (3.7 m) bullwhip. The whip was their badge of office, and, unlike most frontiersmen, they used their fists to settle arguments, rather than pistols and knives.

The trio of bosses did well enough to branch out, but Russell thought they could manage without subsidies. The combination of the sudden end to the Pony Express and the misfortunes of the 'Clean Out of Cash Company and Poor Pay' company led to bankruptcy. The few remaining assets were bought up by Ben Holladay, a genius of sorts, who took over Russell's title of the Napoleon of the Plains, which, though not the most likeable of men, he deserved more.

The barely literate Holladay soon reorganized and improved his purchase to serve new mining towns and frontier communities alike. He believed in regularly inspecting the scene of the action, sometimes driving his own coaches or riding shotgun. He had a specially luxurious Concord coach of his own and on one occasion was held up when he was wearing an $8,000 stick pin under his buttoned up coat and carrying $40,000 in a money belt. The ignorant bandit, whose failure to recognize the great man irked Holladay, got away with a few hundred dollars and a watch and chain. That at least cheered Holladay, who dined out on the story for years.

He lost heavily from Indian attacks on his stations in the aftermath of the Sand Creek Massacre of 1864, and that, plus the fact that he recognized the key role railroads would soon play in the West, led him to sell out to Wells Fargo in 1866. With the proceeds, he went into shipping and railroads, but ran into trouble in 1873, never again to reach Napoleonic status. Meanwhile, Henry Wells and William Fargo went from strength to strength.

Easterners, despite their Western fame, they personified efficiency. Only Wells ever visited the West Coast — very briefly — but theirs was the greatest of all stagecoach networks, moving into railroads, then banking. Today, the firm is part of the American Express Company. Their first office in San Francisco opened in 1852 and they gradually outstripped and outlasted all their rivals. The battle the firm had against crime has been noted. The pair survived panics which engulfed other firms, and by the early 1890s had nearly 3,000 branch offices and delivered over more than 37,000 miles of express routes. California's history, expecially, is closely linked with that of the company.

Rails Across the West

The building of the transcontinental railroad — 2,000 miles from the Missouri to California — was surely the greatest engineering feat in American history. It linked the Far West with the rest of the Union, brought millions to the plains and prairies, and triggered off the building of other railroads. And in human terms it was a stirring, thrilling exploit.

As early as 1832, a railroad to the Pacific was asked for by a Michigan newspaper and the idea caught on, though California was still Mexican. The dream was left to a few visionaries, men like Congressman Benton of Missouri who foresaw emigrants flocking upon a railroad 'as pigeons to their roosts'. New York's Asa Whitney got 16 states interested and, in 1853, army engineers began to survey four different routes. The impending Civil War affected ideas of which route would be best and in the event California remained in the Union ending hopes of a southern route.

The leading visionary was Theodore 'Crazy' Judah, a railroad engineer who thought it absurd to ship engine parts around the Horn and reassemble them in California. During the war, he steered the Pacific Railroad Act through Congress, Lincoln signing it on July 1st, 1862. It was Judah who determined the best route from California and found the hard-headed quartet of local merchants Messrs Stanford, Huntington, Hopkins and Crocker, who would put up the money. Back East, Union Pacific was set up. Yet though ground was broken at Sacramento in January 1863 and at Omaha on December 2nd, the financial position deteriorated. It was a time for fortunes to be made in arms deals, not dreams. 1863 also saw Judah's death and attacks by shipping and stage lines on the would-be rivals.

Fortunately, the ruthless Leland Stanford was now Governor of California, and in July 1865, with the war over and the money raised, the ten year task, that was to take a mere four years, began. Central Pacific had a tough construction boss in Charles Crocker and an equally rugged man in the field, James Strobridge, while engineer and Indian fighter, Grenville Dodge, was Union Pacific's man in charge.

Dodge had an easier time enlisting men, with thousands of Civil War veterans available, and hordes of Irish and other immigrants eager for work. In California, gold was the attraction, silver almost as popular, and hard work in the Sierra a poor third. Many had signed up for a working trip to the mines and found themselves slaving as they never had before.

Against Strobridge's wishes, Crocker decided to replace his workforce with the despised and hated Californian Chinese. Strobridge, most of whose favourite tough Irish workers had deserted him, found to his amazement that the boss was right. Crocker's 'pets' as they were called, proved tough, brave — and sober — workers, cutting through the granite of the Sierra with picks and shovels, blasting powder and, later, nitroglycerin, and using axes, ladders, dumpcarts and wheelbarrows. Behind came other Chinese laying track, becoming so adept that eventually four rails could be laid in a minute. Crocker was soon hiring thousands from China.

Many died during the terrible winter of 1866–67, many lost their pitiful dwellings in killer avalanches, but the indomitable little men beat the Sierra, knowing that Union Pacific had made better time but that they were now faced with the Rockies.

The Union Pacific men — war veterans, Irishmen, some freed slaves, Germans, British and others — never had the nightmare of a killer barrier like the Sierra Nevada, but until Dodge demanded and got troops on a large scale and was given 5,000, there were constant Indian attacks on his men. If

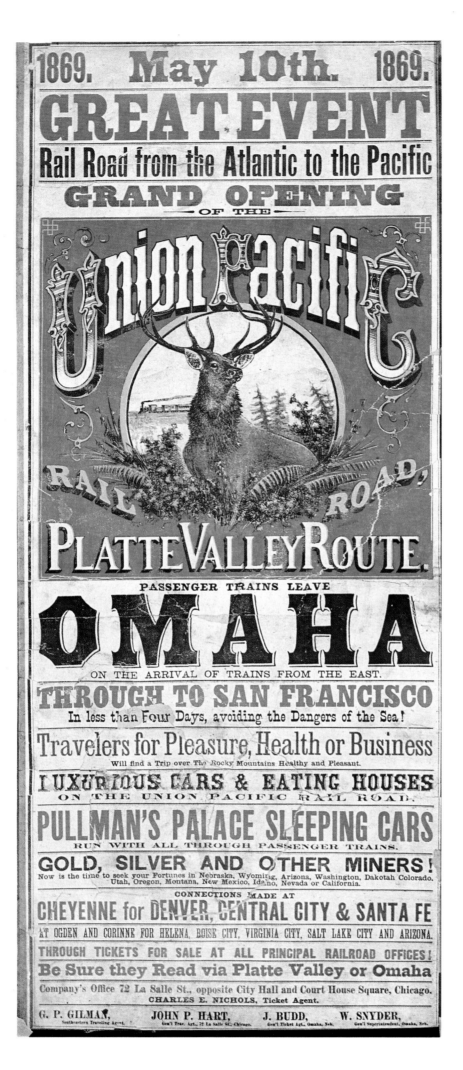

Top right: Chinese workers in action in the Sierra Nevada Mountains in 1867, building the Central Pacific Railroad.

Lower right: Competition between the UP and CP workforces hotted up just before the link-up at Promontory. They overlapped for a while, and blasting charges were a hazard. In the foreground are CP's Chinese workers.

the Indians had fully realized what the railroad would do to their lives, they would have fought even harder against it.

The heart of the operation was the work train behind newly-laid track. Pushed by a locomotive, the lead car was a tool- and blacksmith's shop. Then came three boxcars that served as mobile hotels, next a dining car, and, finally, an administration kitchen and storeroom car. Better remembered are the 'towns' that sprang up at 'end of track', 'hells on wheels' as wild as any Kansas cowtown, though some were to become famous cities like Cheyenne. By contrast, the Chinese camps were as orderly as a fort.

As well as the sheer amount of ground Union Pacific had to cover, and the threat of Indians, the weather, though never as severe as the Chinese endured, could be grim. In the winter of 1866–67, UP had to suspend all operations and the resulting thaw wiped away a full mile of embankment, plus track on either side of a bridge because the snows turned to raging torrents. The bridge survived.

By 1868, the race to span the nation had become a gallop. The Railway Kings/Robber Barons were making fortunes, taking advantage of fat Government contracts and huge subsidies, as well as land grants and loans on easy terms, the key factor being the number of miles of rail built. By 1868, a mile of track was worth $32,000 to each line. It is true that without the Robber Barons the continent would have been spanned later, but the race became insane towards the end with the two lines overlapping and Irish and Chinese letting off blasts of explosives at each other. Finally, President Grant announced that moneys would be held up unless both sides agreed where to

link up. Promontory Point, Utah, was chosen.

Torrential rains held the ceremonies up until May 10th, 1869; it seemed that the whole nation awaited the news, via a telegrapher, that the continent had been spanned by rail. In the event, there was a slight hitch. The spike that had to be hit home had a wire attached to it that would alert the nation when the blow was struck. As a reverent hush descended on the historic scene, Leland Stanford raised a hammer and missed, hitting a tie (sleeper) instead. He gave the hammer to UP's Thomas Durant, but, meanwhile, the telegraphist had sent the signal anyway and the Nation erupted with joy.

Durant was suffering from a headache and he, too, missed the spike, ribald comments and mocking laughter instead of cheers rending the air. Finally, the deed was done.

By 1900, there were four more transcontinental railroads, along with many other routes. That day at Promontory was of colossal importance, black only for the Indians. Now troop trains could rush soldiers to where they were needed, buffalo hunters could get where they wanted more quickly. Buffalo were even slaughtered from the trains.

As for the workers, the truest heroes of the great adventure, they deserve a final paean of praise. Just before the race was over, Dodge's men had laid eight miles of track in a single day. Central Pacific's Chinese, helped by some Irishmen, laid more than ten, sending a locomotive over the completed job to prove to UP observers that it was well and truly laid. So sure of his workers had Charley Crocker been that he had given them an hour off for lunch.

Right: The scene at Promontory Point, Utah, 1869. when the Union Pacific and the Central Pacific were joined – and the continent was at last spanned by rail.

CHAPTER TWELVE
FRONTIER ARMY

Even allowing for the Anglo-American habit of neglecting armed forces down the years in times of peace, the dissolution of American armies after the war of 1812 and the Civil War was the equivalent of a massacre. From over 33,000 in 1815, it had been reduced to under 6,000 by 1821, while after the Civil War, the overall figure for 1866 was 57,072 with a mere 15,000 men responsible for the entire Trans-Mississippi West.

The task of this fragment of what was left of the mighty and victorious Union army was a contradictory one. Troops both protected and fought Indians. They seized their lands when ordered to do so and were also respon-

Below: 'A' Troop, 4th Cavalry, at Silver Creek, Arizona Territory in 1885.

sible for trying to keep interlopers off it. They were the fighting arm of a Government that kept changing its mind about the eternal 'Indian Problem'. Like other soldiers, before and since, they therefore got on with the job. A few remarkable senior officers, notably General Crook and the one-armed Bible-reading General Howard, in their different ways exercised their consciences, while even certain alleged Indian haters could sympathize with the enemy. One wrote:

> *If I were an Indian, I think that I would greatly prefer to cast my lot among those of my people who adhered to the free open plains, rather than submit to the quiet, unexciting, uneventful life of a reservation.*

His name was George Armstrong Custer.

Pre-Civil War soldiers suffered even greater hardships than later ones. This was because communications were that much worse than after 1865. The combination of boredom and lack of promotion amongst officers and men alike led to alcohol being a very real problem. Ulysses S. Grant, serving at a lonely Californian outpost, was one of those who took to the bottle, only escaping a court-martial by hastily resigning. Nine years later, in 1863, his victory at Vicksburg helped change the course of history.

The post Civil War West was divided into the Departments of Columbia, California, Arizona, the Platte, Dakota, Missouri and Texas. In each department were a number of forts, most a cluster of huts built of stone or wood. Few had a second storey, and very few post-Civil War forts had palisades for Indians were too wise to

waste their lives on frontal attacks on stockades. Garrisons ranged from 200 or so to as few as a dozen guarding the overland telegraph. Inevitably, huts were appallingly hot in the summer and many bitterly cold in winter.

What social life there was had to be home-produced. Women were in short supply, while before the Civil War the only white woman an enlisted man could hope to glimpse was the wife of an officer. Early soldiers had often found themselves near friendly Eastern Indian girls in the quite heavily populated forests. In the West, chances of such an encounter were less.

As a result recreation was usually confined to hunting, horse-racing and visits to the crammed sutler's store. Unless there was plenty of adequate local hunting, diet consisted usually of salt beef, salt pork, hardtack – or bread

if the post had a baker – and dried fruit and vegetables. Molasses could be had, as well as coffee and whiskey of varying quality. The sale of liquor was banned on post from 1881, which at once led to off-post 'hog-ranches', complete with whores. Because of the low pay of enlisted men, such services were not always attractive. There were commanders who allowed prostitutes to live in the post, while some of the company laundresses led a double life. This led to the Army witticism that

fort doctors had nothing to do but to confine laundresses and treat the 'clap'. Yet, in fact, most laundresses were just that and were often the wives of N.C.O.'s and other ranks and were respected members of those lonely communities. The conduct expected of an officer and a gentleman on an army post was very high, and any officer indulging in anything more than public flirting was liable to be court-martialled.

The Regular Army fought over 900 engagements with Indians from 1865 to 1898, although many of the 'battles' were no more than skirmishes. By the end of the 1860s, the entire Army was composed of 25 regiments of infantry, ten of cavalry and five of artillery. It was then just under 37,000 men in strength and by the mid-seventies was down to 25,000, most of them in the West.

The pre-Civil War Army had been a predominantly Anglo-American

force, but mass immigration altered its composition. As well as men born in Britain and Ireland, there were many Germans, Swedes, Swiss and other nationalities. At least two Englishmen died with Custer and two serving under Benteen and Reno won Congressional Medals of Honour. There were also ex-Confederate veterans in the Frontier Army.

Cavalry used Springfield carbines and Colt's revolvers in the post-War Army, sabres, though issued, being usually left behind on Indian campaigns. Springfields were the Army issue rifles and carbines from 1873–92, though Sharp's and Remington's breech-loading repeating weapons were among others that were used. Artillery was not used widely. Cochise and his Apaches were startled by it at Apache Pass in 1861 because it was unfamiliar, and rapid-fire Hotchkiss guns were effective at Wounded Knee and against the Nez Perce. Gatling

Left: One of Remington's many fine US Cavalry pictures.

Below: Officers and their families at Fort Walla Walla, Washington Territory, built in 1856.

Guns had no great success, nor did howitzers and mortars in the Modoc War of 1872–73, where they failed to blast the valiant Modocs out of their near-impregnable stronghold.

The men who endured life in the Frontier Army were paid even worse than cowboys, $16 a month in the 1860s, reduced to a miserable $13 in the next decade. As for officers, promotion was pitifully slow. A man who had commanded a regiment in the Civil War, then been reduced to a lieutenant, might take 20 years to reach a captaincy. Officers and men had to endure boredom shot through with moments of extreme excitement and danger. If captured by certain tribes, they might endure a prolonged and agonizing death. As one of their songs put it, they existed on '40 miles a day on beans and hay'.

Though infantry served in every part of the West, the Cavalry was inevitably the principal military arm after the Civil War. In 1865, there were six cavalry regiments, the notorious Seventh being formed in 1866. Of the three later regiments, the Ninth and Tenth were Black regiments, with very high reputations among professionals. Both arms inevitably spent much time building roads, cutting woods and other traditional tasks,

and were needed sometimes for escorting wagon trains.

The '40 miles a day' mentioned above, was of little use against Apache enemies, indeed, without Apache scouts, the wars in the Southwest would have lasted even longer than they did. As we have seen, Indians had fought alongside white men from time to time since almost the beginning of the wars between Red and White. They became even more important in the vast reaches of the West.

As in the East, there was no love lost between certain tribes, as a result of which the idea of a successful all-Indian assault on the whites was even more impossible to achieve than it had been in the days of Pontiac, Brant and Tecumseh. So it came about that Shoshoni and Crow were to help the Americans fight the Sioux and Cheyenne, while defeated Cheyenne were quite prepared to help track down their old allies, the Sioux, in the Wounded Knee campaign. An Indian's freedom to do what he wanted cannot be overstressed, apart from which it was preferable to rotting on a reservation. And above all, Apache scouts were needed to find Apache. Fortunately for the Army, the Apache were never a united nation.

Gradually, a number of white offi-

Above: On the March – The Advance Guard. *By Frederic Remington.*

Left: NCOs of the 1st Infantry at Turkey Springs, New Mexico, during the Apache campaigns of 1885-86.

cers learnt the art of Indian fighting, but, as we shall see, there were always the fools who despised their enemy just as earlier white men had, with catastrophic results. After a catastrophe or, indeed, a victory, the wounded had to face fairly primitive treatment in hospital, if they were got back. Arrow wounds were regarded as more dangerous than bullet wounds because a bullet might go right through the body, whereas an arrow could fragment when it was drawn out. Naturally, far more men died of disease in the West than ever died in battle.

In the 1960s and early 1970s it became fashionable, especially among the ignorant and some rather suspect historians, to denigrate the Frontier Army, despizing officers and men as packs of murderous monsters, and portraying the Indians as peaceloving 'noble savages'. In fact, although only a minority of officers can be claimed as truly sympathetic, and though only fools would expect the ordinary enlisted man to like his foe or even have much understanding of his predicament, the Army's record, despite some incidents that will be examined, was by no means shameful. The well-known atrocity at Sand Creek in 1864 was not committed by regulars but by Indian-hating frontiersmen led by a fanatic. And what could be stronger and finer than General Crook's statement: 'I have never yet seen one "bad" Indian so demoralized that he was not an example in honour and nobility compared to the wretches who plunder him of the little our government appropriates for him', or, Crook again, that scourge of the Apaches, 'During the 27 years of my experience with the Indian question I have never known a band of Indians to make peace with our government and then break it, or leave their reservation without some ground or complaint; but until their complaints are exam-

189

Above: Captain Smith with two Apache scouts.

Left: U.S. Cavalry Column Crossing a Ford. *By Rufus R. Zogbaum, 1885.*

Overleaf: On the Skirmish Line. *By Charles Schreyvogel.*

ined and adjusted, they will constantly give annoyance and trouble.'

'The only good Indian is a dead one' and 'Nits make lice' – to justify slaughtering children – were sayings that survived Frontier after Frontier; as were some of the revenges meted out by Indians. That most Indian wars were started by whites is historical fact, as were the bloody aftermaths. Of course, the U.S. Cavalry image of Remington pictures plus Irish blarney, as shown in John Ford's military Westerns, is historically suspect for the most part, but so is the picture of a bunch of blood-crazed, brutish killers. In the climate of the 1980s it is perhaps at last being realized that the old-time regular army on the Frontier, like its British equivalent in the days of Empire, was, in the main, composed of a bunch of tough professionals simply doing their jobs, sometimes no doubt because they liked action and excitement, but principally because it was their job.

CHAPTER THIRTEEN
WAR ON THE PLAINS

It was the largest gathering of Indians ever assembled on the Plains, perhaps 10,000 of them at Fort Laramie in what is now Wyoming. Among the tribes were Sioux, Crow, Arapaho and Cheyenne, and some of the warriors had only previously met on the battlefield.

Under the guidance of ex-Mountain Man, Tom Fitzpatrick, now an Indian agent a formula for peace on the Plains was agreed. The tribes should neither fight each other nor attack emigrants, whites should be allowed to have roads through Indian land, and the Government should give the tribes annuities and protect them from hostile whites.

The council took place in 1851. In 1854, the Plains Wars began and did not finally end until 1890.

War had almost broken out in 1853, when the commandant at Fort Laramie assumed that an Indian who

Above: Catlin's painting of a Sioux council in 1847.

Left: Breaking through the Circle, *by Charles Schreyvogel.*

had fired at a white was guilty and sent a detail to arrest him. In a skirmish, six Indians were wounded, and only the urgings of the chiefs prevented the incident developing into war. Actual war began over a cow.

A young hothead named Grattan, straight from West Point, knew that all Indians were cowards and boastfully looked forward to proving it. On August 18th, 1854, a settler reported to the fort that a Minniconjou Sioux had killed one of his cows, the Sioux claiming that it had been abandoned. Glory beckoned as Grattan was given permission to arrest the cow-killer in his tent in the Brulé Sioux camp.

Conquering Bear of the Brulé urged the post commander not to send Gratton out until the annual payments to his Indians arrived, when money could be deducted as compensation.

Grattan however, was instructed to act. With 29 men, a howitzer and a mountain gun, plus a French interpreter who loathed Indians, Grattan set off, reached the camp, and discussed matters with Conquering Bear. After half an hour, he lost his temper, ordered his men to open fire, and was himself killed with all but one of his command, who died later. Conquering Bear was one of the dead.

Back East, it appeared that the brave Grattan had been lured to his doom and Colonel William S. Harney at the head of 1,300 men were sent to the Brulé camp – by which time some of the dead chief's friends had avenged him by attacking a stage and killing three whites. By now, extra troops had reached Fort Laramie, whose inexperienced commander was replaced by a Major Hoffman.

When Harney reached the Sioux camp, he demanded that the braves who had attacked the stage be handed over. When Little Thunder, now the Brulé Chief, retired under a white flag, Harney opened fire, 85 Indians being killed and 70 women and children seized.

The wanted men now gave themselves up to prevent further bloodshed, Harney being infuriated when the Indian agent at the fort refused to allow them to be executed. After a year in prison, they were freed.

The Cheyenne were the next to learn about white methods. A dispute over the ownership of some horses led to a confrontation on July 29th, 1857 between some 300 Southern Cheyenne and cavalry under Colonel Edwin V. Sumner. Like others before and after them, the Cheyenne believed what their medicine men had told them – that white men's bullets could not harm them. They learnt the bitter truth, or, rather, half of it, for Sumner had his men charge with their sabres, which the medicine men had not mentioned. At least they realized that fighting white men bore little relation to their own concept of war, which has been described earlier.

An uneasy peace followed, but hordes of gold seekers, heading through Indian territory to Colorado created a tension which, happily, did not lead to war. Many a miner had cause to bless Indians who helped lessen the dangers of the trail. The Sand Creek Massacre was six years away.

The next crisis occurred to the east in Minnesota. Although most of the Sioux and Cheyenne had been driven to the Plains to Wisconsin and Minnesota in the late 18th century by Ojibwa who possessed French guns, there were still 'woodland' Sioux, the Santee, in Minnesota. They were

Right: The Indian Council *by Seth Eastman, painted c.1849.*

farmers now, rather than hunters, but their farmlands had shrunk as whites poured into Minnesota. In 1860, they were confined to reservations along the Minnesota, not in itself a disaster, but made so because of a few particularly corrupt officials and traders. These wretches, who were to cause so many white deaths, defrauded the Indians of their treaty money. Two bad harvests in succession only made things worse.

In 1861, many troops left Minnesota to fight in the Civil War, few officials realizing the growing dissatisfaction among the Indians. None were angrier than Little Crow, a Christian who had visited Washington and lived in a house in white man's clothes. In July 1862, the Santee, having endured a grim winter, found that their payments had not arrived. Agent Galbraith called for troops, whose commander so sympathized with the Indians that he refused to fire at them after they had broken into a warehouse. Galbraith promised Little Crow that supplies would be issued to other Santee 35 miles away, but in front of a big band of Sioux Galbraith gave in to the traders who refused to issue any supplies. One Andrew Myrick called: 'So far as I am concerned, if they are hungry, let them eat grass, or their own dung!' The Santee departed.

Little Crow's position was tragic. He knew there was no defeating the whites, yet his men wanted war. On his next visit to church he shook hands with white friends for the last time.

Above: Frederic Remington's Return of the Blackfoot War Party.

Left: The Santee Sioux, enflamed by ill-treatment, massacred hundreds of whites in Minnesota in 1862. Here are some of the survivors.

When some Santee burst into his room that night and told him how they had killed some settlers while looking for food, he was called a coward when he still spoke for peace. It was then that he gave in.

Among the first to die was Myrick, his throat filled with grass. An appalling uprising followed, the desperate Sioux killing several hundred men, women and children in a rebellion that recalled Pontiac's. Little Crow knew that the key to success was Fort Ridgeley, but could not persuade his men to take it at once. Instead they ravaged New Ulm for its loot. When the fort was reached, a small artillery detachment under Sergeant John

Jones was ready for them. Despite amazing valour under artillery fire unmatched in the history of the Indians Wars, and bitter hand-to-hand fighting when reinforcements managed to reach the fort, the Santee were forced to retreat.

Now, 1,400 men under Colonel Henry Sibley were marching towards the Sioux, who were finally crushed at Wood Lake. Three hundred and nine Indians were sentenced to death, but the Bishop of Minnesota, to the fury of his flock, hastened to explain the cause of the uprising to Abraham Lincoln. The President decided that only proven murderers and rapists should hang. Thirty-nine did so on December

26th, 1862 to tumultuous cheers. Those Sioux who were not imprisoned were driven westwards to a worthless Dakota reservation.

Six months later, Little Crow was spotted and killed by a hunter. His son was captured and was reprieved, being only sixteen. Later, he became the founder of the Young Men's Christian Association among the Santee.

Massacre at Sand Creek

In Colorado, despite pressure from white miners, the only fighting was traditional warfare between rival tribes. But in 1861, Black Kettle of the Southern Cheyenne as well as other

Above: The notorious 'Reverend' Chivington of Sand Creek ill-fame.

Left: Charles Russell's painting of Cheyenne Indians returning from a horse-stealing raid.

chiefs signed away some Cheyenne and Arapaho land in return for an Arkansas River reservation and training in farming. The authorities made the usual mistake of thinking they had made a treaty with entire peoples. This recipe for disaster was made worse by the personalities of two ambitious men, Governor Evans of Colorado and the infamous Methodist minister, Colonel John Chivington. With most regulars fighting in the East, this man of God with military ambitions was in virtual charge of the Denver area.

Some horse-stealing, possibly by Cheyenne, gave him his chance to order all Cheyenne found to be killed — so one of his officers later stated — and soon most Cheyenne were on the warpath, except for Black Kettle and his band, though some of his wild

young braves killed a family called Hungate, whose deaths – and bodies – caused an uproar in Denver. It was mid-1864 and Chivington's plans were prospering.

Then, to the minister's annoyance, Black Kettle returned some white captives. With his political and military ambitions, he wanted war, not peace. His Third Colorado Cavalry were 100-day militia so he had to act fast. Black Kettle had the kindly Major Wynkoop at Sand Creek with him and knew he and his people were safe. What he and the major did not know was that the area was being sealed off from interference, and that Wynkoop was to be replaced by one of Chivington's own men. A few honourable officers tried to argue with Chivington and were cursed. 'Kill and scalp all big and little. Nits make lice,' reminded Chivington with oaths. So it came about that Black Kettle's camp was attacked by 700 men, a few of them regulars, and artillery. One hundred and twenty-three Indians were killed, two-thirds of them women and children. Chivington was later to claim that he fought 700 warriors, killing almost 600.

Bravery was not sufficient for the Indians, for there were too few warriors in camp. Men, women and children were hacked to pieces, many of their limbs being displayed in Denver to great acclaim. Black Kettle was among those who escaped, for many of the militiamen were not only undisciplined but suffering from hangovers.

Even men who were usually regarded as Indian-haters were appalled by Sand Creek. A Congressional committee was shocked, Kit Carson called the killers cowards and dogs. But the militiamen had all left the service and could not be touched. The old frontier belief that to kill an Indian was never a crime still held firm, so Chivington survived – but little more. When he attempted to enter politics, shouts of 'Sand Creek' rang out and he failed to get elected.

Naturally, the rejoicing settlers were the ones to suffer most, for now the full fury of the Plains Indians erupted. The amazing Black Kettle still spoke for peace, but it was the fighting chiefs who were heard in

Sioux, Arapaho and Cheyenne camps. One war party came upon nine of Chivington's veterans, heading for home. After all had been killed, the Indians found who they were from Cheyenne scalps in their baggage and hacked their bodies to pieces. Innocent settlers, and ranchers died, too, while Northern and Southern Cheyenne came together for war, and the Cheyenne, though their language and customs were different from the Sioux's, became friends and allies.

Above: The great Sioux leader, Red Cloud, who led the Sioux and Cheyenne to victory in the Powder River War of 1866-68 – 'Red Cloud's War'.

Opposite page: A thrilling painting by Charles Schreyvogel.

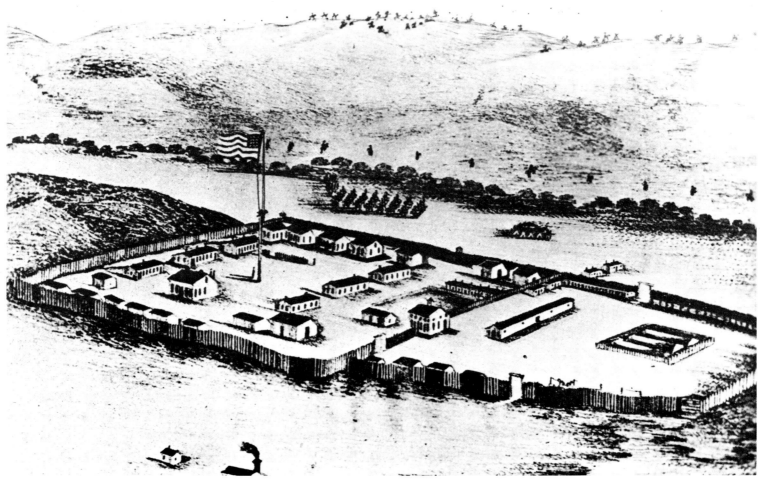

The War the Indians Won

When the Civil War ended in April 1865, more troops became available for service on the Frontier. They were badly needed.

In the East arguments raged as always about the Indian Question. Some wanted them turned into farmers and taught other skills, others wanted the fighting tribes destroyed, not necessarily by Sand Creek methods, but destroyed all the same in the sense of being confined as quickly as possible on reservations or killed. 1865 saw plenty of action in the Powder River country of Wyoming through which John Bozeman had pioneered a trail to the Montana goldfields. The year ended with the area, a favourite hunting ground of the Sioux, still in their hands.

In March 1866, the great Sioux leader Red Cloud of the Oglala agreed to sign a peace treaty as long as Sioux land was untouched. In May, a huge council of Sioux and Cheyenne was held at Fort Laramie, Red Cloud bringing 1,000 braves with him, but insisting that they await yet more Sioux. At that moment, Colonel Henry Carrington was marching to the fort with 700 men of the Eighteenth Infantry, including wives and children, the object being to build forts along the Bozeman Trail. Though halting some way from Fort Laramie, the whites were spotted by a 'friendly' Brulé named Standing Elk, who warned Carrington there would be trouble. When Peace Commissioner Taylor arrived, peace prospects were vanishing fast, Red Cloud making a fiery speech then stalking out and striking his camp. Others followed him.

Carrington marched on, short of the new breech-loading Spencer Carbines, but with four guns and two famous ex-Mountain Men, Jim Bridger and Jim Beckwourth. Troops were left at Fort Reno, built earlier, and on July 13th at the forks of Piney Creek Carrington ordered Fort Phil Kearny to be built. On August 3rd, men were sent up the trail to erect Fort C.F. Smith.

The Indians constantly harassed operations at Phil Kearny, the wood detail being a special target, while more and more Indians joined Red Cloud, including rising comets like Sitting Bull, Gall and Crazy Horse. Few whites completed the Bozeman Trail that summer.

Carrington had spent the Civil War at a desk and, though quite able, thought more about building than training his 'green' troops. His officers, knowing nothing of Indian-fighting, wanted instant action. Extra troops appeared until Carrington had ten officers, three doctors and 389 men. Several more officers rode in, one of them, Captain Fetterman, destined to create a catastrophe.

Carrington was under orders from General Cooke to hit the hostiles in their winter camp. Cooke knew nothing of conditions on the Powder River. However, there was action on December 6th, Fetterman leading 30 men to save the wood detail. He was a fighting fool who used to boast: 'Give me 80 men and I'll ride through the whole Sioux Nation.' This time he was

Left: Fort Phil Kearny, scene of ferocious fighting in the Powder River War.

Right: Chief Wahakie and the Shoshoni sided with the whites against their enemies, the Sioux and Cheyenne.

Overleaf: Charles McBarron's portrayal of the Wagon Box Fight of 1867.

Below: Raiding Party *by Charles Russell.*

lured down a valley until the enemy turned and killed two of his men. When Carrington arrived the Indians rode away – to plan the next encounter. For Fetterman, it showed that they were indeed cowards.

On December 21st, he learnt the truth too late. There were between 1,500 and 2,000 warriors waiting for the wood train that morning, ten decoys, including Crazy Horse and the Cheyenne Little Wolf, leading them into a trap. The wood detail came under fire at 11 am and Carrington fatally allowed Fetterman to lead the rescue party, the latter pulling rank over another officer. He had asked for 80 men, and 49 infantrymen, 2 civilians and 29 cavalrymen under Lieutenant Grummond gave him just that.

The decoys pretended fear when Carrington sent a shell toward them and they led Fetterman and his command over a ridge and out of sight. In a battle of less than an hour, the whole command was wiped out because of Fetterman's folly.

Carrington expected a frontal attack, not knowing that Indians rarely did so, especialy in winter conditions so severe that food was their principal concern. The occupants of the fort did not have the comfort of that knowledge. Word was sent to Fort Laramie by two riders, John 'Portugee' Phillips and a man named Dixon. It is only legend that 'Portugee' rode alone the 238 miles on the Colonel's horse – only an idiot would have taken a solo mount – but he did put a stop to all Christmas night revelry. The Indians, who allegedly attacked 'Portugee' on his ride, were now in camp awaiting the spring.

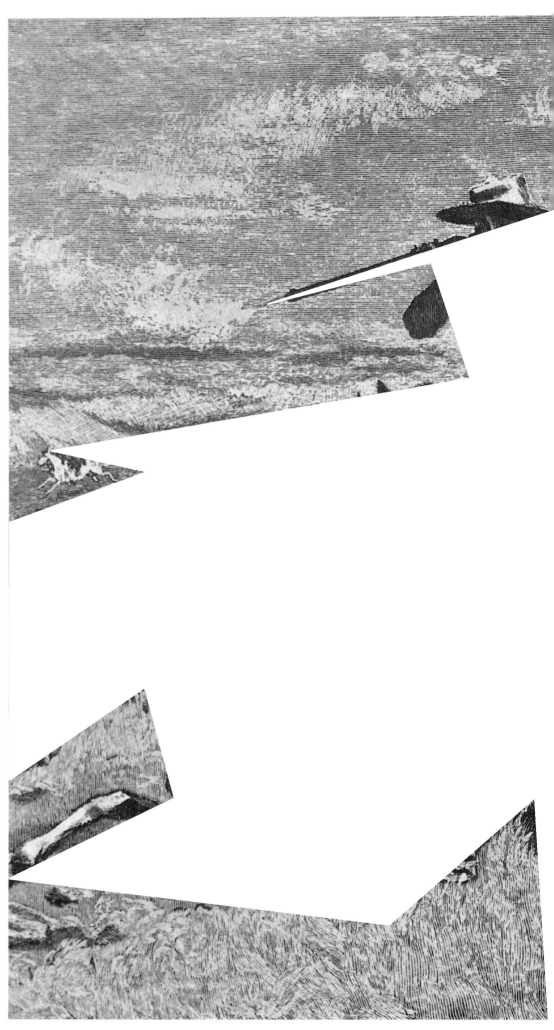

Remington's Plainsmen *in action.*

While General Sherman, in charge of the Department of the Missouri, thundered about extermination, and Carrington was transferred, even though an abler leader might have done little better, a peace council was planned for April at Laramie, negated because the leaders who counted were absent. Meanwhile, the Union Pacific tracks were heading westwards and needed guarding, especially as the Indians were furious that their friends the buffalo were being slaughtered to feed the track-layers. When, as we have seen, the UP workers met those of the Central Pacific in Utah in 1869, it was another catastrophic blow to the tribes, for now troops could be rushed to endangered positions.

The Indians were still masters of the Powder River country in 1867, but now white technical skill led to disaster. In July, 800 warriors, most of them Northern Cheyennes swept down on a mere 20 soldiers and 12 civilians hay mowers near Fort Smith, driving them into a corral. The troops had the new Spencer repeaters and metallic cartridges, however, and when a relief party arrived, they found that only three of the defenders had been killed in a six-hour battle.

The following day, Sioux under Red Cloud attacked woodcutters near Fort Phil Kearny, some reaching the fort, 32 holing up in a wagon-box corral. It was the same story. Valiant but useless Sioux charges, then a retreat when a relief column quickly appeared. Some 60 Sioux lay dead.

Yet there was no real chance of the army defeating the Indians at this time, even though conditions would soon be in the white man's favour. The Government gave in early in 1868, leaving the Powder River country in Indian hands. The hated forts were abandoned, to be burnt by the victors. On November 6th, the great Red Cloud rode into Fort Laramie ending his victorious war. Though he spoke for his people in the West and, memorably, in Washington, he had fought his last fight. A sad, handsome figure, he lived on until 1909.

Countdown to the Little Bighorn

While Red Cloud's war had been raging, the Southern Plains had been in a turmoil – as were the authorities in Washington. Many, even outside the Indian Bureau, sympathized with the Indians, but army officers and Westerners did not, resenting that authority was split between army and civilian agents.

General Sherman ordered General Hankock to show the flag south of the Arkansas, the only result being that a major war was made more certain. A typical ensuing incident was the destruction of an empty village. The resulting Treaty of Medicine Lodge in 1867 gave the Southern Cheyenne and Arapaho one reservation and the Kiowa, Kiowa-Apache and Comanche another. There will be more about the Kiowa and Comanche in the next chapter. Meanwhile, all except legitimate whites were kept off the reservations and the dream of turning Indians into farmers lived again.

It was too good to last. Promised arms and ammunition failed to reach the Cheyenne and young braves were soon on the warpath. Hankock's replacement, Civil War cavalry hero, Phil Sheridan, decided on a winter campaign while the Indians lacked food and their horses were weak.

The instrument was to be the Seventh Cavalry under George Armstrong Custer. A major general of volunteers at the age of 26 in the Civil War, this ambitious cavalryman was certainly a glory hunter, but he did not hate Indians, being not unlike them himself, and, as has been noted, he made it quite clear that if he were an Indian he would be a 'hostile', not a reservation dweller. He was a harsh commander but survived being court-martialled for an amazing list of offences, so that he was ready when Sheridan chose him to lead the offensive.

Black Kettle now re-entered history, still preaching peace from his camp beside the Washita River. He could not control all his young men, as he had admitted to the local commandant at Fort Cobb, Indian territory, but his camp was peaceful enough.

To it in late November 1868 came Custer at the head of 800 men. Nearing the village on the night of November 26th, he split his command into four groups ready to make a dawn attack. Black Kettle, meanwhile, was hoping to return four white captives that he held.

He never stood a chance. The Seventh charged at dawn. He and his wife were killed, and, despite the valour of men and women, there could only be one result. Friendly Arapaho joined in the action, cutting off the regiment's second-in-command – Major Elliott and 19 men – but even when Comanche and Kiowa appeared on the scene, the Seventh was still master of the situation, retiring safely back to Sand Creek; but it brought no credit on the army, for most Cheyenne had wanted peace. Inevitably, many women and children had been killed in the ferocious action, while the Seventh's morale was lowered by the fate of Elliott and his men. Many felt Custer should have gone to his rescue.

The Southern Cheyenne split after this disaster, the warrior society known as the Dog Soldiers going north to join the Northern Cheyenne. Those that survived a sudden attack by Major North and his Pawnee scouts linked up with their cousins.

Meanwhile, the Sioux were split between those who wanted war and those, like Red Cloud and Spotted Tail, who believed that words must now save their people. Most Indians however, continued their old life that was so soon to vanish, and listened to rising stars, above all the Hunkpapa Sioux Sitting Bull. He was by now the dominant figure of the Sioux Nation, even compelling the admiration of Northern Cheyenne and Arapaho braves. There were other heroes at this

Left: The long column advancing through the Black Hills is Custer's 'scientific' expedition of 1874. A gold rush followed.

Above: One of many Indian delegations to Washington. Standing: John Bridgeman. Seated, left to right: Red Dog, Little Wound, Red Cloud, American Horse, Red Shirt.

Left: A vivid photograph of a brave enduring the Sun Dance ordeal.

Right: Chief Standing Bear's picture of Custer's Last Stand.

time of crisis, most notably the inspired young warrior, Crazy Horse, and the Cheyenne Two Moon, but Sitting Bull was warrior, religious leader and politician, a man who ranks with the greatest leaders of the Indians' past.

The Black Hills were the sacred heartland of the Sioux (though they had once been dominated by the Cheyenne). They had found gold there, but their friend, Father de Smet, and equally friendly traders, had told them to keep the finds secret. In 1874, however, Custer and ten troops of the Seventh, plus infantry, Indian scouts, scientists, engineers, miners, newspapermen and a photographer entered the hills, the miners giving away the true purpose of the expedition. The resulting gold finds electrified the nation. Soon prospectors were taking the 'Thieves' Road', as the Indians called it, despite efforts of the Army to keep them out.

The Government tried to buy the hills. Red Cloud demanded $70 million and 200 years of support, while Crazy Horse simply said: 'One does not sell the earth on which the people walk.' As the number of prospectors multiplied that winter, the Government ordered all Sioux to be back on their reservations by January 31st, 1876, all those not back to be regarded as hostiles. The winter was so appalling that year that even those who were prepared to go in often failed to make it, while the Army could only launch one campaign in such weather, and that was a failure.

At a great council in April 1876 in the valley of the Tongue River, Sitting Bull told the assembled Sioux, Cheyenne and Arapaho: 'We are an island of Indians in a lake of whites. We must stand together or we will be wiped out. The soldiers want war. We will give it them.'

The whites were planning a three-pronged attack. General Terry and Custer advanced from the east with 925 men, 700 of them the Seventh Cavalry. There were three companies of infantry, a detachment with three Gatlings, and 40 Arikara scouts. They left Fort Abraham Lincoln, Dakota Territory, on May 17th, while Colonel Gibbon and 450 men were heading eastwards and 1,000 men under Crook marching up the Bozeman. Gibbon's job was to cut off Indians driven north by General Crook, who had made his name fighting Apaches in Arizona.

Sitting Bull and the Hunkpapa held a great Sun Dance in June in the enormous camp of the Sioux, Cheyenne and Arapaho. At the climax of it, Sitting Bull had a vision of soldiers coming down from the sky like grasshoppers, their heads down and their hats falling off. The soldiers were falling into the Sioux camp and no one doubted what the vision meant. Victory would be theirs. It was June 14th. Custer had 11 days to live.

Beside a stream that flowed into the Little Bighorn, some 15,000 Indians, 4,000 of them warriors, pitched five tribal circles and a Cheyenne one, some Arapaho companions lodging with the Cheyenne. The fighting began on June 16th when Crook's command was hit by 1,000 Indians as it rested beside the Rosebud. The battle lasted six hours and was Crazy Horse's day. At last, the Indians fought as one, not as soloists in a great game. Though Crook claimed a victory, he retreated as fast as he could with his wounded and stayed put until reinforced, so missing the grand climax of the campaign.

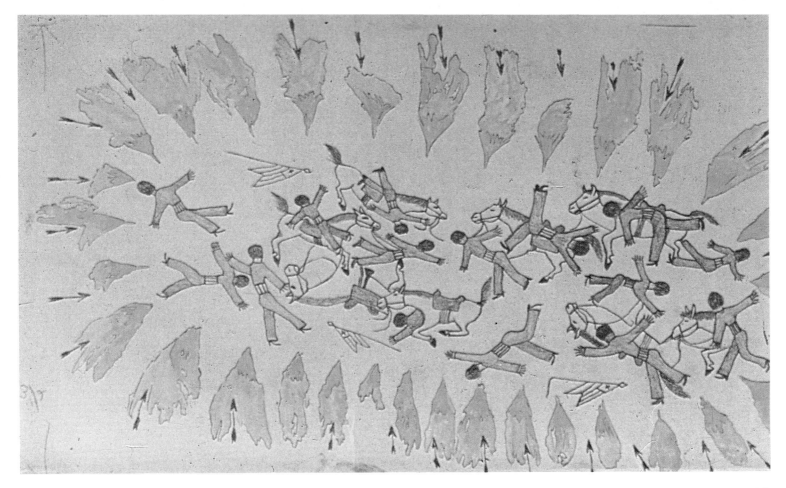

The Cheyenne call the Rosebud 'The Battle Where the Girl Saved her Brother'. Chief Comes-in-Sight was leading a charge when his horse was shot from under him. Death seemed certain, when a horse and rider raced to cover his body. Moments later, he leapt up behind the rider, his sister, Buffalo-Calf-Road Woman.

After the Rosebud, the Indians celebrated their victory. Terry, knowing nothing of Crook's defeat, was aboard the *Far West* steamboat on the Yellowstone, Gibbon having just arrived. Major Reno, second-in-command of the Seventh, was sent to reconnoitre and found empty camp sites, not knowing that the Rosebud action was in progress. Going farther south than he should have, he saw signs of a huge trail, only to be upbraided by Terry who feared he might have been spotted. Custer was ordered up the Rosebud and down the Little Bighorn from the south, where Crow scouts had seen smoke. Gibbon was ordered across the Yellowstone by ferry, then up the Bighorn to the Valley of the Little Bighorn, which he was to descend from the north. Terry assumed that Custer would fight a battle and that Gibbon could deal with fugitives.

Just how much leeway Custer was given in case the unexpected happened will be argued about until the West loses its appeal. What critics of one or more of the commanders sometimes fail to remember is the size and determination of the Indian army, as well as the superb ability of its leaders.

Custer set off on June 22nd with over 600 men, plus six Crow scouts, leaving his Gatlings behind, believing they might slow him down. The Seventh's divisive problems since the Washita had not been resolved and morale was low. Custer had almost missed the campaign having been too frank back in Washington about crooked traders at army posts and their corrupt bosses. President Grant's brother was one of the accused and only Custer's record got him back to the West. On June 23rd, he forced the pace without realizing he was heading through a huge circle of camps. Only his Crow started to realize the danger.

The Indians knew soldiers were

near on the 24th, though not who they were. Sitting Bull was on a hilltop praying for victory; Custer was telling his Arikara scouts that he would one day be President – and he followed the Indian trail he saw, instead of going up the Rosebud, a change of plan that a victory would have excused. He reckoned to attack on the 26th, when Gibbon's men would be in position.

Indian villages were seen by scouts the next day some 12 miles away. Fearing the hostiles might run, Custer divided his command with fatal results. Captain Benteen was sent south with 125 men, Major Reno ordered ahead with 112 to hit the southern end

of the camp. A troop was ordered to escort the pack train and Custer with 215 men started for Ash Creek, now Reno Creek.

Seeing some dust ahead and thinking the Sioux were running, Custer ordered Reno to attack, promising support.

The Indian encampment was an idyllic spot that morning, with boys swimming in the river and women gathering wild turnips. Most of the warriors had firearms, some of them Winchesters, others had bows and clubs. Dust proclaimed Reno's approach and women and children ran as they charged firing. Sioux warriors

Above: Sleeping Bull holding a cavalry saber.

Left: Matthew Brady took this fine study of George Armstrong Custer.

Right: Sitting Bull, the most famous of all Sioux leaders and one of the greatest of all Indians.

mounted and covered their families escape.

Four miles away, the Cheyenne saw the gunsmoke and prepared to fight. Two Moon had a glimpse of the soldiers being driven back by Sitting Bull's adopted son Gall and his braves. The troopers were fighting on foot for better accuracy, but were soon forced over a small river where they dug in on low hills. Sitting Bull was surprised that so few had charged until he realized that they had expected to be supported. None knew which whites were attacking them.

Custer had seen the start of the charge from the hills above. He sent Trumpeter Martini back to ask Benteen for more ammunition. Martini was the last man to see Custer and his 215 alive. No one ever knew just what happened to them in the desperate fight of less than an hour, for gunsmoke covered the field. However, some facts are clear. The Indians

melted away from the Reno fight when he had lost half his men, having heard that more soldiers were heading towards their camp. Reno was pinned down so Gall sent men to combat the newcomers. They headed for the Little Bighorn and Custer's men fell back on a high ridge, to be attacked by waves of warriors under Crazy Horse and Two Moon.

The doomed men made their last stands in smaller and smaller groups until all were dead. The Indians did not know who had attacked them until near the end, and though several claimed to have killed Custer, nothing was ever proved. He had had his hair shorn, which made recognition more difficult. Two of his brothers and a nephew also perished.

Benteen reached Reno and both heard heavy firing. Though Reno was to be made the scapegoat, he could never have saved Custer. As it was, the soldiers were pinned down until the

next morning, when the Indians suddenly rode away, having heard that more troops were approaching.

Nothing was left alive on the Custer battlefield except Major Keogh's horse Comanche, and in all 265 whites were dead or mortally wounded. It was the greatest Indian victory since 1792.

When the news reached the American people a surge of anger swept the nation. Those Indians who had stayed at peace were in despair as their lands were swiftly annexed. The Sioux were banished to a new reservation, where, said Red Cloud, 'There are a great many bad men and bad whiskey.' Meanwhile, soldiers headed West by rail and, the victors, facing food shortages with winter coming and the buffalo almost gone, faced a grim future. Space does not permit the recounting of the full aftermath of victory. Crook achieved the only victory, hitting the camp of Chief American Horse. General Nelson A. Miles caught up with Sitting Bull, who

managed to escape to Canada with many of his people the following May, many others having crossed the border earlier. Though fighting continued sporadically, finally even Crazy Horse gave up the struggle. In May 1877, he led 1,000 men, women and children into Camp Robinson, Nebraska and threw his three Winchesters at Crook's feet.

He was too potent a force to be trusted, and the atmosphere at the fort became more and more tense, with Indian set against Indian, and, finally, on September 5th, 1877, while a Sioux held him, a white guard stabbed him mortally. He had drawn a knife so was 'resisting arrest'. He died that night, aged only 35, leaving behind him an immortal legend.

The Flight of the Northern Cheyenne

The remnants of the Northern Cheyenne were rounded up and sent south in 1877 despite the promise of a northern reservation. Nine hundred and thirty-seven of them reached a wretched desert-like reservation in what is now Oklahoma in mid-1877 and soon many were dying of fever, and their children of the dreaded 'coughing sickness'. They had a good agent named Miles and a friend in Lieutenant Lawson, but they seemed doomed to extinction.

They actually warned Miles that they were going to escape, but as on their journey they had seen the new railroads, the telegraph wires, the floods of settlers, he did not believe them. But on September 9th, 1878, 284 Cheyenne, only 87 of them warriors, started for home in Montana.

Their fighting retreat was one of the West's greatest epics, for they fought battle after battle with troops, cowboys and settlers, led by their chiefs, Dull Knife and Little Wolf. Finally, they reached Nebraska, where Dull Knife said he would stop. 'Nothing evil has ever happened to us here,' he said. Little Wolf did not agree and the band split amicably, Dull Knife taking 45 warriors, 61 women and 42 children with him, Little Wolf, 40 warriors, 43 women and 38 children.

In October, Dull Knife's band was surrounded as they tried to reach Red

Opposite page, top: The widely used way of carrying a baby by Indians, these pictured being Cheyenne.

Opposite page, below: Dull Knife (seated) and Little Wolf, the leaders of the Cheyenne who escaped north from Indian Territory in 1878.

Right: Northern Cheyenne prisoners at Dodge City.

Cloud or Spotted Tail. They were told that as the Sioux leaders had been taken north, the best solution for the fugitives was to come to nearby Camp Robinson. They agreed to, but carefully disassembled their best weapons. The women put the barrels under their clothes and tied mechanical parts to moccasins and beads to make them seem to be ornaments. Old weapons were kept intact and handed in the next morning when the expected order came, the Indians only being allowed their knives.

In the hut in the fort that was given to them they hid their weapons under the floorboards. They were promised a transfer to Red Cloud's camp, but nothing happened. A new commandant, Captain Wessels, then arrived at the Fort, suspicious of the Cheyenne and eager to move them south again. The Indians replied that they would kill each other rather than return.

On January 3rd, 1879, they were told to prepare to go south at once. When they refused, they were imprisoned without water, food or fuel in their hut. When Wessels finally said that women and children could leave the hut, the Cheyenne said they would all stay together. Iron bars were then placed on the hut's doors.

That night the Cheyenne assembled their weapons, painted their faces, and prepared to die. At 10 o'clock, 130 Cheyenne, 44 of them men and boys, erupted out of the hut that Wessels had thought was impregnable, hurling themselves through windows and firing as they came. Dead and dying soldiers provided more guns. As troops, many of them half-dressed, poured out of their billets, the Cheyenne were covering the retreat of the women and children outside the gate. The braves could have escaped, but the idea of leaving the women and children was unthinkable.

The fighting retreat lasted from January 9th until the 21st. Finally, there were 35 Cheyenne trapped in a hollow some 35 miles from the fort. They had been attacked by infantry, cavalry and artillery and were now almost out of ammunition and were singing their death songs. They would not surrender.

There came a moment when it seemed that all were dead, but, suddenly, three warriors, all drenched in blood, erupted from the pit and and began to charge. One had an empty pistol, the other two grasped knives.

They charged straight at 200 men until a hurricane of fire brought them down.

The soldiers found 23 dead in the pit and only two unwounded Indians, both women. Dull Knife and some others had escaped to the Pine Ridge Reservation, but would the captives and wounded at Camp Robinson be allowed to join them, or would they be forced south? Happily, so moved were Americans when they heard about the Cheyenne epic that the survivors were allowed to settle down with the Sioux and, finally, return to their beloved Montana home. There they were re-united with Little Wolf and his band.

Their adventures had been less epic. Having hidden in Nebraska for the winter, they had been found by an old friend, Lieutenant Clark, who told them what had happened and how the whites had wanted justice done. The army had always admired the Cheyenne as fighters and many now became valued scouts. Times had changed and life was difficult for the Cheyenne, and difficult it remains. Yet they were and are back home, while their epic flight remains unique in the annals of the West.

CHAPTER FOURTEEN

SOUTHWEST AND NORTHWEST

When Texas ceased to be an independent nation in 1847 and became a state of the Union, much of it was still Indian country. The two most famous tribes were the Kiowa, some 2,000 strong, and the 20,000 strong Comanche Nation. What the smaller tribe lacked in numbers it made up for in fighting spirit.

In 1834, the Kiowa had made a sensible arrangement with Colonel Henry Dodge that they would cease attacking wagons bound for Santa Fe in return for trade concessions, and for more than a decade there was peace on the great trail. The warriors instead concentrated on attacking encroaching Texans to the south. Then came the Californian Gold Rush, bringing thousands across Indian land – and bringing cholera that devastated the small tribe.

The Colorado strikes of the late 1850s increased the tension until, under Chief Little Mountain, the Kiowa began fighting the Americans. When troops were withdrawn to the east at the outbreak of the Civil War, the Santa Fe Trail became suicidal once more, and when news of Sand Creek broke, the Kiowa and Comanche took ferocious revenge on the whites.

The Kiowa, with a few Comanche allies, were defeated by ex-Mountain Man Kit Carson and his New Mexico Volunteers in the Texas Panhandle in November 1864. The whites had Ute and Apache as allies, but what beat them was Carson's two 12-pounder howitzers. Soon they were on a reservation which included their favourite buffalo range. The whites promised them tools, clothing and food. But the buffalo herds were shrinking fast and reservation life proved joyless. The tribe split into those who wanted peace and those who longed for war.

Satank, the leading warrior, was now too old to be the tribe's principal chief, Satanta being given the honour. He was prepared to extract what he could from the Americans, but not to give up traditional raiding, while Kicking Bird was the choice of the peace party. To satisfy everyone, or so it was hoped, Lone Wolf, a centre candidate, was chosen.

At the great council at Medicine Lodge, Kansas, in 1867, there were as noted Kiowa, Comanche, Cheyenne and Arapaho. It resulted in the Kiowa and Comanche being given a smaller reservation, but hunting rights north of the Washita River were retained and $25,000 a year was allotted them for useful goods.

That was the reasonable deal, too reasonable for the military, General Sherman persuading President Grant to remove the hunting rights. What money the Indians did get was often late. Once again the tribe split, Satanta advocating war, Kicking Bird, though a famous warrior, still wanting peace. He was called a coward at the 1870 Sun Dance and had to prove himself, doing so spectacularly by leading a raid into Texas and charging at the head of his band against men of the Sixth Cavalry. After impaling a trooper on his lance, he was listened to more respectfully.

The next year, a war party left the reservation again under Satank, Big Tree and the prophet, Sky Walker. A less than efficient seer, he told his companions not to attack officers in an open coach protected by just 17 men, for soon there would be better pickings. So they failed to kill one of their most deadly enemies, General Sherman! The next day, a wagon train was attacked, and one man was tied to his wagon, his tongue cut out, and he was burnt to death.

Shortly after this, Satanta admitted to a Quaker agent at the Kiowas agency that he had led the raid. He told the agent the many wrongs done to the tribe, but his confession was passed on to Sherman, who ordered the chiefs tried for murder.

There followed a series of events as glorious and ghastly as any in Indian history. Satank, Satanta and Big Tree were put in an open wagon to be taken

away from their people. Old Satank suddenly started singing, ducking his head from time to time under a blanket. The song he sang was his death song, the song of his warrior society, the Society of the Ten Bravest, and in between his chanting, he was gnawing the flesh from his hands until he could slip his handcuffs off. Under the blanket there was a knife, hidden in his clothes perhaps, or slipped to him by a friend. He would never see the inside of a white man's prison.

Suddenly, he leapt up, knifed one

Above: Trails-the-Enemy and his wife, a typically handsome Kiowa couple.

Opposite page: The great Kiowa chief, Kicking Bird.

Overleaf: Holding them off, a Currier and Ives lithograph.

guard and seized another's carbine. Just before he could fire, the officer in charge shouted an order and the other guards fired. When he died, they flung him into a ditch and the wagon moved on. Satanta and Big Tree were tried in Jacksboro, Texas, sentenced to hang, but, to the dismay of Indian-hating frontiersmen present, given imprisonment with hard labour in Huntsville Prison. They were freed – to the fury of Sherman – when Kicking Bird and Lone Wolf – a particularly hostile chief, swore to keep the peace.

It was an impossible promise. With the slaughter of the buffalo reaching its climax and more and more whites invading Indian territory, Kiowa, Comanche, Cheyenne and Arapaho could not be contained on their reservations. Sherman struck at the hostiles, Kicking Bird restraining most of the Kiowa from joining them. There was no resraining Satanta and Big Tree, but even they at last gave in. Satanta was sent back to Huntsville

and hurled himself head first from the prison hospital window. Big Tree still had the will to live. Meanwhile, the unfortunate Kicking Bird was ordered to select the most recalcitrant Kiowa for shipment to prison at Fort Marion, Florida, and he held back those he considered would most help the tribe in the grim times to come. Sky Walker, chosen for Florida, warned him that he would not live long and Kicking Bird did indeed die soon after. An army doctor stated that the cause of death was strychnine poisoning.

The Kiowa endured three years in Florida and were then returned to the West, the tribe settling in Indian Territory. Big Tree settled down as a deacon and a Sunday School teacher.

The Lords of the South Plains

In his *Travels in the Great Western Prairies*, published in 1839, J.T.

Right: Cynthia Ann Parker, mother of the great Quanah Parker, with her daughter, Prairie Flower.

Below: A Kiowa Village by Baldwin Mollhausen.

Farnham described the Comanche as the 'Spartans of the Plains', praising their 'incomparable horsemanship', their 'incredible courage' and their 'unequalled rapidity with which they load and discharge their firearms'. He also warned how their enmity made them 'more dreadful than that of any other tribe of aborigines'.

The Comanche, who had no principal chief, were generally regarded as the finest horsemen in North America. They were implacable enemies of the Americans who came to Texas. There was no room in a Comanche camp for a male captive, so most Texan prisoners were killed. Women might be raped, and might be married into the tribe, while children were likely to be adopted into it.

A Comanche gave no quarter, but he expected none, yet a white man who proved courageous might be treated well. Torture was by no means inevitable.

Perhaps the most famous Comanche captive was Cynthia Ann Parker, who was taken into the tribe when she was nine, not long after Texas became independent. She soon became a Comanche and married one named Peta Nocona, furnishing the tribe with three children at a time when its birthrate was perilously low. One was Quanah Parker, greatest of all the Comanche leaders.

These incomparable horsemen could ride 100 miles without rest or food. They always had fresh mounts ready and they planned for retreat as well as attack. It was to combat them that the Texas Rangers were raised, as well as to protect their vast frontier.

When Texas joined the Union in 1847, infantry were sent to man newly-built forts, an absurd miscalculation; however, cholera was to help the whites more than any troops could, the disease crossing the Plains with the Forty-Niners.

Cynthia Ann Parker was recaptured

Above: A buffalo hide yard in 1878 at Dodge City. The destruction of the buffalo played a key part in destroying the Indians' way of life and ability to resist.

Left: Quanah Parker, the most famous Comanche Chief. Unlike so many Indians, he successfully made the transition from war to peace. He was a friend of Teddy Roosevelt.

by Rangers in 1860, young Quanah never managing to find where she had been taken. Finally, at the Medicine Lodge Treaty of 1867, he learnt that she had tried repeatedly to escape to her Comanche people, starving herself to death after her daughter died in 1864.

In 1871, 31-year old Colonel Ranald S. Mackenzie, highly regarded by President Grant, was given command of the Fourth Cavalry at Fort Richardson, Texas, and rapidly turned the regiment into the finest cavalry outfit in the army. Tough discipline was his watchword, but not spit and polish, and he made his men into guerilla troops fit to match the Comanche. In March 1872, he defeated the Kotsoteka Comanche who settled on a reservation, then he sought to destroy the New Mexican arms and whiskey traders known as Comancheros, who supplied the Comanches with arms and whiskey in exchange for plunder. He broke their power, but Quanah and his band were still at large.

In 1873, an army of buffalo hunters descended on the Texas Panhandle,

turning it into a gigantic slaughterhouse. For now, with a Sharps rifle, a single hunter could kill more than 200 buffalo a day. Soon there would be no buffalo left as the Indians, surrounded by rotting carcasses, saw only too clearly. Needless to say, the Government made no effort to keep the hunters out, while the military rejoiced. Their work was being done for them.

Now, a hard core of warriors – Comanche, Kiowa, Arapaho and Cheyenne – decided on revenge. They were encouraged by a Comanche Medicine Man named Isatai, the type of prophet, as we have seen, whom Indians too often turned in time of crisis. This one had predicted both a comet and a drought; now, so he claimed, he had been to heaven and could belch up wagon-loads of ammunition. He also claimed that the Indians and their horses would be immune from white men's bullets. Victory would mean the return of the buffalo.

The target was to be a trading post called Adobe Walls on the North Canadian River, which the buffalo

225

Left: A Stagecoach Fighting Off Indians *by Charles Schreyvogel.*

hunters used as a base. To this Quanah Parker led 700 warriors of four Indian Nations, with Isatai announcing that he would stop all the white men's guns.

There were only 28 men and one woman at the post, lodging in three buildings some way from each other. Though their rifles were superb, a successful surprise attack could have wiped them out. Accounts vary as to why the Indians failed to achieve that surprise, but the failure was fatal, and the warriors soon found that Isatai was a liar. Time and again they charged at the post, but the hunters buffalo guns with telescopic sights played havoc, and, finally, the Indians retreated. Quanah forbade the flogging of the prophet, considering his disgrace punishment enough.

The whites stuck 13 Indian heads on poles, how many others had been killed being unknown as the Indians took away the bodies. Only three defenders were dead. Though

Quanah's valour had been noted by all, and though he was never blamed for the defeat, Indian morale was badly bruised. Texas and Kansas suffered as a result as hundreds of braves sought bloody revenge. Colonel Mackenzie, leading the hunt for Quanah Parker, failed to find him, but came across the huge Palo Duro Canyon which few whites had seen since Coronado's time. It was shelter for Kiowa, Comanche and Cheyenne and their families, but Quanah Parker was not there or there would doubtless have been sentries guarding the hideout. As it was, the troopers swept down into it, destroyed the Indians' winter food and dwellings, and rounded up their huge – and vital – horse herd. The fact that many Indians escaped was not serious, for now the end was near and it came finally when Quanah Parker led his band into Fort Sill in the Fall of 1875 and came face to face with Mackenzie.

The rest of Quanah's story is a

Below: A Southern Cheyenne family, *with a travois holding a cage for a child.*

happy one. In his remaining 35 years, and without ever losing face, he triumphed in peace as he had on the warpath. There were difficult years at first, but he became an expert on land deals, having learnt to speak English well. He also traced his white relations, even studied farming with them, then returned to the Comanche.

He lived in a fine house and had eight wives; he became a friend and hunting companion of Teddy Roosevelt, riding in his innaugural procession. In 1911, he was buried beside his mother dressed as a chief of the Comanche Nation.

Captain Jack

The appalling fate meted out to California's Indians has been briefly noted in Chapter Eight. One tribe alone was able to stage a genuine war against the whites – the Modoc. Unlike most Californian Indians, they were a warrior race. They lived in northern California in the Tule Lake country, and in the 1850s much of their best land was annexed. There was no war at this time because the young chief Kintpuash thought it better to try coexistence with the interlopers; he rather admired them. The newcomers gave him the name by which he is remembered – Captain Jack.

During the Civil War, with tensions growing between the Modoc and the Americans, the tribe was forcibly moved to the Klamath Reservation in Oregon. The local Indians did not want them and the Modoc were not supplied by the Government. So they went home. Although the authorities had no objection, the local whites resented their return and spread ru-

Left: A group photograph of the Modoc War. From left to right top are O.C. Applegate, Toby Riddle, who tried to bring about peace and her husband Frank. Seated are Modoc women.

mours about them, until the unfortunate Modoc were once more told to head for Oregon. In November 1872, troops of the First Cavalry came to remove them, a fight took place, and the Indians escaped to lava beds below Lake Tule which came to be known as Captain Jack's Stronghold. They are now a National Monument, a monument to valour.

The stronghold was a natural fortress with some grass for the Modoc cattle and nearby water from the lake. In the fortress were some 250 Modoc, perhaps 60 of them warriors. Jack had hoped to be left in peace, but a band led by Hooker Jim had killed settlers on the way and on January 13th, 1873, troops arrived to flush the Modoc out.

It took them until May to do so, by which time the Indians had killed 82 soldiers and civilians for the loss of only five Modoc. Divisions in the Modoc camp were to prove fatal, while the murder of General Canby, a sincere friend of the Indians, under a flag of truce, was even more disastrous to the Modoc cause, as it enraged the nation. In the end, the tribe fragmented and the despicable Hooker Jim gave in, promising to track Jack down. They did.

After a trial which he and three other Modoc hardly understood, and during which Hooker Jim, the villain of the piece, gave evidence against the leader who had genuinely sought peace, Captain Jack was hanged. His courage never failed him. While the rope was being put around his neck, a settler called: 'Jack! What would you give me to take your place?' 'Five hundred ponies and both my wives!' he shouted in reply.

More than 1,000 troops had fought the Modoc. Robert A. Murray, author of the definitive *The Modocs and Their War*, states that considering the number of Indians involved, this was the most expensive Indian war that the United States ever fought. It was also the only one in which a general was killed by Indians.

The remaining 153 Modoc were sent to Indian Territory, the survivors who wished to being allowed to settle in Oregon in 1909. As for their dead leader, his body had been dug up after the hanging and appeared at carnivals in the East at 10 cents a look.

230

Joseph

The Northwest saw a number of bitter wars in the years before the Civil War, which cannot be described here, but before considering the most famous of the later wars, a quotation from General Crook's *Autobiography* indicates the unenviable plight of the Indian-fighting Army. He served in the Northwest as a young officer and made these observations:

> *It was no infrequent occurrence for an Indian to be shot down in cold blood, or a squaw raped by some brute. Such a thing as a white man being punished for outraging an Indian was unheard of . . . The trouble with the army was that the Indians would confide in us as friends and we had to witness this unjust treatment of them without the power to help them. Then when they were pushed beyond endurance and would go on the warpath we had to fight when our sympathies were with the Indians.*

Few except the settlers who wanted his people's land have failed to sympathize with Chief Joseph of the Nez Perce, the handsome, advanced tribe that had never killed a white man. Indeed, they had welcomed every one of them from the time of Lewis and Clark. Joseph's band lived in the beautiful Wallowa Valley where Idaho, Oregon and Washington meet. Tension had been mounting since the mid-1850s because of miners, settlers and the treatment handed out to individual Indians. Then, in 1863, the valley was 'given' to the government, meaning that settlers would now stream in. Joseph's father, until then a Christian and a friend of the whites, tore up his New Testament.

He died in 1871, young Joseph replacing him. He was about 30 and his Indian name, Hinmaton-Yalaktit, meant Thunder Rolling in the Mountains.

He refused to move when ordered out of his valley, asking President Grant to intervene. He did, and part of the valley remained Indian.

In 1875, the Government went back on its promise and prominent Nez Perce argued whether to fight or to try yet again to live in peace. Though they chose peace, it would only need one incident to cause a war. The appearance of the one-armed 'Christian General', Oliver Otis Howard, as the new commander of the Department of the Pacific should have spelt peace, for his record as a friend of Blacks and Indians was a good one. Alas, he was over-fearful of a general Indian uprising and confused the Nez Perce love of their land with a militant cult sweeping other parts of the Northwest which was indeed militant and anti-white. He informed Washington that Joseph and his band must be moved to the Lapwai Reservation to join the rest of the tribe.

Though Joseph felt he must submit, he was shaken at a meeting in May 1877 on being told that his people must move within 30 days. Their

Opposite page: The Nez Perce leader, Chief Joseph, not the Red Napoleon of legend but a great human being.

Below: A modern Nez Perce with a coup stick.

stock could not be rounded up in that time, while the Snake River was dangerously high to cross. Howard was inflexible.

After a difficult crossing of the swollen Snake River during which many mares, calves and cows were lost, the Indians settled near the reservation boundary to await the expiry of the deadline in ten days. They were joined by other bands of Nez Perce. Arguments raged as to what should be done until three young braves went on a rampage and killed four Indian-hating whites. As Joseph and his brother Ollokot tried to restore order, 16 other young braves killed 14 or 15 whites before starting a drinking and looting spree. The heartbroken Joseph knew that flight was now the only hope for his people.

It was a flight through some of the most mountainous country on the continent, a 1,700-mile epic which was to see 2,000 troops plus Indian scouts and civilian volunteers trying to catch the fugitives. The first action – after Joseph had made a last attempt at peace – saw less than 70 warriors whip over 100 First Cavalry and some civilians, 34 soldiers being killed and a mere three Indians wounded. On July 6th, Joseph was joined by the bands of Chiefs Red Echo and Looking Glass, bringing his force up to some 150 warriors and 550 women, old men and children.

The retreat was organized by a council of Indians, Looking Glass being the most notable fighting chief, while Joseph was the inspirational and political figure. He was not the 'Red Napoleon' of legend – a legend partly due to the whites' failure to understand Indian leadership, and partly because the humiliations that the whites suffered seemed less shaming if they were up against a Napoleon. Joseph's job was seeing to the safety of the women and children and it was his task to organize the camp.

After a short rest, the Nez Perce marched on until on July 11th they were suddenly attacked by artillery. In a two-day battle, which Howard was to claim as a victory, while admitting that the Indians fought as well as any troops he had ever seen, the Nez Perce lost far less than the 23 men that Howard claimed, and carried out a

'masterly, deliberate and unmolested retreat', according to one of Howard's officers. It helped that the Nez Perce's accuracy with rifles was far more deadly than any other tribes' – in the opinion of their opponents.

Looking Glass seems to have wished that the fugitives should find a home with the Crow or, failing that, with Sitting Bull's Sioux in Canada, several thousand being there almost a year after the Little Big Horn. Whatever the final choice was, Montana was reached after more rugged marching. They were faced by 35 soldiers,

Opposite page: Chief Ouray of the Ute, who attempted to live in peace with the whites. He lost his lands.

Below: Ambitious General Nelson A. Miles reached the top of the Army, not without controversy.

200 volunteers and some Flathead Indians at a roadblock in the Bitteroot Valley. The commander, Captain Rawn, wanted action, the volunteers did not, and the Nez Perce went through. On August 9th they were surprised by Colonel Gibbon and more than 200 men and though they beat off the Americans, women and children died – some of the women in action.

With Howard once again on their tail, the Indians crossed Yellowstone National Park, recently created as the first such park. Looking Glass was ahead sounding out the Crow, but they were firm allies of the U.S. Army. It was clear that Canada must be their objective.

Their position was becoming desperate, especially as they were slowed down by their sick and wounded. And now the rising star, Colonel Nelson A. Miles was heading from Fort Keogh to cut them off. A tremendous battle raged 40 miles from the Canadian border, Miles calling his enemy the best Indian marksmen he had ever seen. Their skill and tactical sense was such that they killed seven sergeants of the Seventh Cavalry. But the end was near. The great retreat ended on October 5th, 1877. Joseph's brother was dead, Looking Glass and other leaders were dead. Joseph surrendered to Miles. What has always seemed the most magnificent of all surrender speeches, culminating with the words, 'From where the sun now stands I will fight no more forever', has been exposed by Colonel Mark Brown (*Montana*, January, 1972) as the invention of Howard's aide, Captain Charles Erskine Scott Wood, but what he wrote in *Century Magazine* in 1884 is moving enough:

It was nearly sunset when Joseph came to deliver himself up . . . Pressing around him walked five of his warriors their faces were upturned and earnest as they murmured to him; but he looked neither to the right nor the left, yet seemed to listen intently. So,

234

the little group came slowly up the hill to where General Howard with an aide-de-camp, and General Miles waited to receive the surrender. As he neared them, Joseph sat erect in the saddle, then gracefully and with dignity he swung himself down from his horse, and with an impulsive gesture threw his arm to its full length, and offered his rifle to General Howard. The latter motioned him towards General Miles, who received the token of submission.

Those present shook hands with Joseph, whose worn and anxious face lighted with a sad smile as silently he took each offered hand, then, turning away, he walked to the tent provided for him.

Joseph surrendered just over 400 Nez Perce, a quarter of them warriors. Ninety-eight warriors and some 200 women and children had escaped to Canada where Sitting Bull and his Sioux made them welcome. Meanwhile, Miles's promise that the Nez Perce could stay at the military post on the Yellowstone for the winter then return to Lapwai, was broken by General Sherman, despite the fact that

most Americans, even Westerners (excluding the new inhabitants of the Wallowa Valley) were on the side of the Nez Perce. When they passed through Bismarck, Dakota Territory, the captives were cheered and Joseph given a banquet. Then they were imprisoned, first at Fort Leavenworth, Kansas, then at other places in the state, many dying of malaria. Many more were to die in Indian Territory, where they were finally sent, but the scandal was such that the Government finally repented. In 1885, the 268 surviving Nez Perce went back to the Northwest, only 118 to Lapwai, the rest to a reservation in Washington State, including that public danger, Chief Joseph, a national hero except in his own homeland. He died in 1904 – according to the agency doctor, of a broken heart.

The Apache Wars

'No Indian has more virtues and none has been more truly ferocious when aroused. . . . For centuries he has been pre-eminent over more peaceful nations about him for courage, skill, and daring in war; cunning in deceiving and evading his enemies; ferocity in attack when skilfully planned am-

buscades have led an unwary foe into his clutches; cruelty and brutality to captives; patient endurance and fortitude under the greatest privations. . . . In peace he has commanded respect for keen-sighted intelligence, good fellowship, warmth of feeling for his friends, and impatience of wrong.'

So wrote Captain John G. Bourke in his classic *On The Border with Crook.* Like his chief and other officers who knew the Apache as men and not just as enemies, he held them in high regard. The average Arizonan of his day, however, regarded them as lower than vermin.

The reasons for this contradiction went far back into history. Their reputation was even more lurid than that of their Navaho cousins, who, after years of bitter struggle, then exile, were allowed to return to at least part of their homeland in 1868. Surprisingly, it was grim General Sherman, no sentimentalist where Indians were concerned, who was so appalled by the Navaho's place of exile at Bosque Redondo, that he sent them back to their Canyon de Chelly, where Kit Carson had defeated them in 1864 – and destroyed more than 500 peach trees.

Right: Timothy O'Sullivan's photograph of Apache poised for action.

Opposite page, top: Young Lieutenant Bascom was a key figure in the events at Apache Pass in 1861 which led to the long war with Cochise.

Opposite page, below: Government pack mules near the Mexican border in 1883.

In 1864, the Apaches were on the verge of becoming world famous, so much so that Parisian hoodlums adopted their name. Yet why were the Apache so ferocious, so fiendishly cruel? Centuries of strife make it useless to try and find out who triggered off the conflict, Spaniard or Indian, but it is fairly clear why the Apache became so cruel and implacable.

First, their women and children had been enslaved by Spaniards and Mexicans for generations, and when the Americans came to the Southwest, enforced prostitution was added to the list of infamy. Apache women could inflict hellish tortures on captives, yet their extra savagery may well have been not just for menfolk lost but for children as well. In a single incident in 1871, 29 were stolen from them. As for mutilation of the dead, it is surely significant that the practice became far more widespread from the 1860s onwards. Ironically, when the Apache first met Americans they welcomed them as friends. They could hardly be worse than the Mexicans, so the Apache must have reasoned. Chihuahua in Mexico passed a law in 1837 that offered the equivalent of some $100 for a warrior's scalp, half as much for a woman's and half that for a child's. Scalphunting was an old trade, but never on this scale. Which is not to

deny that Mexicans had every reason to hate Apache.

There were some 6,000 Apache in the mid-19th century, a disunited nation whose bands were prepared to fight against each other. Their name means 'enemy' in Zuni. What are now Arizona and New Mexico were their principal homes, though they roamed far more widely. The most famous of all the Apache, the Chiricahua, lived in south-east Arizona.

As fighting men, they have rarely been equalled. An Apache could achieve 70 miles in a day on foot. The legendary powers of endurance of an Apache warrior were developed when he was a boy. His sister was expected to swim and run, while he did the same before sunrise throughout the year, then, at daybreak, he had to run up a hill and down again with a mouthful of water. This taught the youth to breath correctly through his nostrils.

The Apache used bows, lances, clubs and knives, sometimes poisoning their arrows. They were always short of ammunition, which may account for their alleged lack of accuracy with firearms. It did not prevent them from keeping the Southwest in a state of panic, while their ability to live like lizards in their dramatic land added to their power to terrorize and amaze. They aimed at none of the heroics of the Plains tribes, preferring stealth and ambush. When trapped with their families their courage was ferocious. If there had been more of them, the Apache Wars might have lasted into this century.

The first great Apache leader to fight against the Americans had longed for their friendship. He was Mangas Coloradas, who had survived an appalling massacre of Apache by Mexicans, organized by an American scalphunter named James Johnson in 1837. The victims had been lured to a feast, where the Mexicans killed a disputed number of them. Mangas, born in the 1790s, and well over 6 feet (1.8 m) tall, extracted terrible revenge, so terrible that by the time the Americans came to the Southwest in 1846, northern Mexico was a land of death and desolation.

The invading Americans refused Mangas's offer of an alliance, but his power was growing without their

help. One of his daughters married Cochise of the Chiricahua, whose fame was already considerable. His father-in-law's wish to befriend white men did not survive a brutal flogging by miners because the giant Apache had dared to watch them working. Cochise seemed to be having more success in establishing friendly relations with the Americans – though he still led raids into Mexico – when in 1861, he was wrongly accused of kidnapping the stepson of a rancher named Ward – a boy who was to grow up to be the noted interpreter-scout, Mickey Free. Young Lieutenant George Bascom accompanied Ward on a trail that led to Apache Pass.

Left, top: General Crook with two of his Apache scouts, Dutchy (left) and Alchise.

Left, below: The young and confident John Clum, agent of the San Carlos reservation, flanked by Diablo and Eskiminzin.

Below: Apache scouts with their white commander, probably Lieutenant Maus.

There, Cochise met the white men in Bascom's tent and told them that Coyotero Apache had the boy. The inexperienced Bascom told Cochise that he and the Apache with him would be interned until the boy was returned, at which the enraged chief cut through the tent with a knife and ran through a group of soldiers outside it. Though he escaped, the Americans held his men. He returned the next day with a large force.

Apache Pass was on the Overland Stage route. Over the next week there were conferences, skirmishes, attempts to bargain on each side by use of hostages, and the deaths of most of the hostages. The outcome was 25 years of almost constant warfare. There could never have been complete peace in the Southwest, but Bascom's treatment of a chief who had been friendly to Americans and a potential ally was catastrophic in its results. He was to be killed in a battle in New Mexico between Union and Confederates a year later, little knowing the havoc his inexperience had wrought.

It was a good time for the Apache to take the offensive, for the Civil War played into the Apache's hands. The few remaining settlers made for Tucson, acquired, as noted, by the United States in 1853 as part of the Gadsden Purchase that added southern Arizona and New Mexico to the nation. The only setback the Indians had was at the Battle of Apache Pass in 1862 when they were faced with artillery for the first time. The Apache commanders were Mangas and Cochise, the former being wounded in the battle.

The shot that felled him was fired by Private John Teal, who had been cut off from the rest of the troops and was prepared to sell his life dearly, shooting over his dead horse. To his astonishment, the fighting ceased when he brought the huge Apache to the ground. Teal simply walked away. Meanwhile, Mangas was carried to a Mexican village where a doctor was told that if his Apache patient died, the town died too. Fortunately, he survived and was soon back with his people.

He was now about 70 and the thought of peace seemed good to him. He could not know that General

239

Carleton and his Californian Volunteers, whom he had fought at Apache Pass, wanted the Apache wiped out, as did nearly every other white in the territory. He was lured into the camp of Captain Edmund D. Shirland under a white flag, captured, and rushed to an abandoned fort. There, General Joseph E. West told Private Stocking of the California Volunteers: 'I want him dead or alive tomorrow morning, do you understand? I want him dead!'

Mangas had two guards that night, who heated their bayonets and tormented him with them. Finally, he had had enough. He was not a child to be played with, he said, and they shot him. It was claimed that he had been trying to escape, that he had taken on seven soldiers, etc. They scalped him, cut his head off, boiled it, then sold the skull to a phrenologist.

The result was an even greater nightmare in the Southwest, Cochise, now grimmer than ever, leading the fight, while new names came to the fore, Geronimo, a Mimbres Apache, and Victorio of the Warm Springs band. Regulars replaced the Volunteers when the Civil War ended in 1865. They had no more success, prompting Sherman's famous remark: 'We had one war with Mexico to take Arizona, and we should have another one to make her take it back.'

Despite the endless war, Arizona's population was increasing, for miners, settlers and ranchers were prepared to take the risk. Meanwhile, the number

Left: Apache scouts with two Apache prisoners in leg-irons.

of Apache inevitably decreased. Cochise was beginning to long for peace, but an appalling massacre of Indians who had settled down at Camp Grant made that impossible. There were some 500 Apache there, mostly Aravaipa. Their chief, Eskiminzin, once a warrior, proved a fine leader of a thriving community. However, Indian-hating citizens of Tucson and those doing well out of army contracts had other ideas. Alleging that some of the Apache were still raiding, they assembled a murderous gang of Mexicans and Apache-hating Papago Indians, plus six Anglos and, as leader, a lawyer and ex-Indian fighter named Oury. In a welter of murder, rape and mutilation perhaps 125 Indians were killed, a mere eight of them men, and 30 children were carried into Mexico to become slaves. No-one was found guilty at the subsequent trial to the fury of President Grant and most of the nation. It was the old story.

This was the climax of a policy of extermination. Better policies were on the way.

General Crook arrived in June 1871 to be commander of the Department of Arizona. Later, he was to be a leading champion of the Apache, and already he was honest as well as tough. He hired Apache scouts to track Apaches, and was ruthless in tracking down hostiles, though women and children were never harmed. Indians had to be on the reservation.

Meanwhile, Cochise was longing for peace, and thanks to his remarkable friendship with frontiersman Tom Jeffords, it came about. Films and books have portrayed their blood brotherhood. Jeffords had arrived in Arizona in 1862 when the Cochise war was at its height. Having organized a mail service between Tucson and Fort Bowie, he found that his riders were on virtual suicide missions. So he went to see Cochise in his stronghold, an even more suicidal mission whose sheer valour paid off. Cochise agreed to let the mail through and the two men became blood brothers. It was Jeffords, the one white man Cochise would trust, who, in 1872, brought the deeply religious General Howard, who could speak for the President, to Cochise. The result was glorious.

There would be peace. The Chiricahua would have a reservation in the mountains that bore their name and a valley beyond, and Jeffords – much against his will – would be their agent.

In 1874, the great Chiricahua died, Jeffords being the only white man who knew where he was buried. Cochise's sons, Taza and Naiche, persuaded Jeffords to stay on, but now, with Cochise's influence gone, renegades penetrated the reservation, and raids on Mexico began again. To the joy of every Indian-hater in Arizona, the Chiricahua were ordered to leave their beloved home and go to the huge San Carlos reservation, unhealthy for mountain Apache and containing Apache who were their enemies. Taza died on an official trip to Washington, and his people were removed, Jeffords, bitter at the treachery, being eased out of his position. He died in 1914.

Many Chiricahua slipped away, some to other bands, some to freedom in the Sierra Madre mountains of northern Mexico. The rest were 'concentrated' – the new policy – at San Carlos.

For a time the reservation was well-run by a brash 22-year-old named John Clum, who had a high but justified opinion of himself and of his Apache police. By 1877, he was boasting that he could handle every Apache in Arizona, but was not given the chance and resigned to found the famous Tombstone *Epitaph*.

San Carlos was now badly run. Outbreaks, bloody and expensive to deal with, became regular. Victorio terrorized both sides of the border until he was trapped and killed in 1880 in Mexico. A year later, the 70- or so year-old Nana went on a six-week raid that began with 15 braves and continued with 40. He killed over 30 while eluding hundreds of civilians and 1,000 troops. There seemed no way of containing these greatest of guerillas. A treaty between Mexico and the U.S.A. in 1881 helped, for it allowed troops to cross the international border in pursuit of hostiles, but the raids went on.

General Crook returned and raged at the conditions at San Carlos. He would fight hostile Indians, but fought corrupt whites, too, who did

Apache posed beside the prison train taking them to exile in Florida in 1886. Geronimo is seated second from the right in the front row.

their best to smear him. It was Crook who was faced with the Geronimo outbreaks. A medicine man rather than a chief, he came to the fore partly because Cochise's son Naiche was not ambitious. His considerable fame was – and is – due to the massive newspaper coverage of the final outbreaks, besides which he had a powerful personality.

Not that Geronimo was alone in staging outbreaks. In November 1884, not long after Geronimo's second escape in two years, a warrior named Ulzana with a mere dozen men covered 1,200 miles in four weeks. They killed Apache scouts when they could, and their families, ambushed a cavalry troop, stole horses constantly to keep on the move and vanished into Mexico having killed 38 men and lost just one.

Washington had now come to the conclusion that the Chiricahua and the equally belligerent Warm Springs Apache must be removed from the Southwest. Sheridan came West to preach the new gospel – and to object to the use of Apache scouts – despite that fact that only they could find the hostiles, they and a few brilliant young officers of Crook's, and the legendary Chief of Scouts, Al Seiber. After the last major outbreak ended in 1885, Crook had promised Geronimo and Nana that if they came in and spent two years exile in the East, they would be allowed back to Arizona. It seemed that the wars were over, but just before the Chiricahua reached the border, an American bootlegger got the Indians drunk, told them lies about what would really happen, and set off the last Apache 'war'. Geronimo and Naiche had 16 warriors, 13 women and six children with them. Meanwhile, Sheridan reprimanded Crook harshly and accused his scouts of treachery. He promptly resigned, and the ambitious General Nelson A. Miles took over. He did not believe in Apache scouts, but was finally forced to use them. The only one of Crook's key young officers to be used by Miles was Lieutenant Gatewood, and it was he who, with two scouts, found Geronimo and Naiche south of the border. He gave them Miles' message – to surrender and go to Florida with their families and await the President's decision, otherwise they would be fought to the bitter end. The Apache Wars ended shortly after at Skeleton Canyon on August 25th, though officially the end came when Miles arrived on September 3rd. On the 7th, Geronimo's band were put aboard a train for Florida.

Miles gave no credit to Gatewood, but what he did to the Apache was far worse. The two scouts who had found the hostiles were sent to Florida, as were Crook's always loyal scouts and, in all, 381 Chiricahua and Warm Springs Indians. Thirteen Indians on a delegation to Washington were detained on their way home and sent into exile. True, the Chiricahua were now hated in Arizona and the whites wanted them banished for ever, but this was treachery. One 'Broncho' Apache proved that defeat was not an Apache concept when he managed to escape from the prison train just before it reached St. Louis. He returned to Arizona and fought a one-man war for many years until he was finally killed. His name was Massai.

Meanwhile, many Apache were dying in Florida because its climate was so unsuitable for them. Later, all were sent to Mount Vernon Barracks, Alabama. They were not forgotten. General Crook visited them, as did John Clum, and a campaign was launched to allow them to return to the West. Arizona would not have them but in 1894 they were sent to Fort Sill, Oklahoma, which suited them better than Florida, being in the West. None got back to Arizona, however, except Eskiminzin and his band. The rest were given the choice in 1913 of staying where they were or joining the Mescalero Apache in New Mexico, where the majority finally went.

Geronimo had one last moment of glory when, with other Indians, including Quanah Parker, he rode in Theodore Roosevelt's Innaugural Procession. It was 1901, and some army chiefs were appalled to see such a killer on parade in Washington. Teddy Roosevelt, a true Westerner from his ranching days, though born in the East, simply wanted 'to give the people a good time'. Geronimo gave them just that, getting a reception surpassed only by the President himself. Later, he was to ask if the Chiricahua could return to Arizona. The answer was no. Arizonans, understandably enough, did not want them back. He returned to Fort Sill, where he died in 1909.

There were greater Apaches than Geronimo, the headline grabber, but on the subject of 'bad' Indians it is best to let General Crook have the last word: 'I have never yet seen one so demoralized that he was not an example in honor and nobility compared to the wretches who plunder him of the little our government appropriates for him.'

CHAPTER FIFTEEN
THE END OF THE FRONTIER

Just when the story of the Old West, American or Wild, ended is hard to determine. The Superintendant of Census in 1890 had no doubts, stating that the country's 'unsettled area had been so broken into by isolated bodies of settlement that there can hardly be said to be a frontier line', a statement that startled many who had never considered such a thing happening.

In 1893, Frederick William Turner read his famous paper, *The Significance of the Frontier on American History* to members of the American Historical Association in Chicago, in which he explained how the European heritage of Americans accounted only for similarities between European and American society and that to explain previously neglected differences his-

torians should look to the distinctive environment of the United States.

Particularly significant was the area of free land on the western edge of the advancing settlements, said Turner, who concluded with the ringing words, 'the frontier has gone, and with its going has closed the first period of American history'.

It took some time for Turner's

doctrine to spread, let alone become gospel, and, though not swallowed whole today, gospel it remains. Yet the Frontier lingered on – in spirit at least – for a few more years, and in some areas it was still more than somewhat lively.

For the purposes of this book, one can only indicate signs of the times. In 1902, Butch Cassidy and the Sundance Kid, who, with other members of the Wild Bunch, had enjoyed a lucrative career robbing banks and trains, headed for South America. That the pair were almost certainly not killed at the famous shoot-out so vividly shown in the classic Western about them is all to the good, for Butch certainly deserved to get home to the West. Despite leading a gang of ruthless men, he never killed anyone on either side of the law in the United States.

As late as 1912, there was an old-style train robbery in the West, the villains being Ben Kilpatrick, alias the Tall Texan and late of the Wild Bunch, and one Nick Grider. Alas, Ben was no longer the star he had been in his prime 'dynamite days'. Express messenger David Trousdale first distracted him, then battered his brains out with an ice pick. Then he finished the less distinguished career of Nick Grider with a shot from the Tall Texan's rifle.

One badman managed to span Old and New West in a suitably symbolic way. Henry Starr, a relation by marriage to Belle, the 'Bandit Queen', had quite a successful career as a badman – in between spells in prison from 1892 onwards. He once took part in a double bank raid in Stroud, Oklahoma, successfully attacking the town's two banks. Having started his career on horseback, he ended it in an automobile. He and three others

Opposite page: The ruts made by wagons on the Oregon Trail can be seen to this day in several states. These are in Oregon itself.

Below: the classic photograph of (part of) the Wild Bunch, which proved of great interest to Pinkerton detectives. From left to right – Top: Bill Carver and Harvey Logan, alias Kid Curry. Sitting: Harry Longbaugh (the Sundance Kid), Ben Kilpatrick (the Tall Texan) and Robert 'George' Leroy Parker, better known as Butch Cassidy.

drove to a bank in Harrison, Arkansas, in 1921, having discovered the delights of driving, not riding, to the scene of their crimes some time earlier. It was not his lucky day. Bank President Meyers had had a door put in the back of his vault and there was a loaded shotgun in place. Meyers used it to inflict a mortal wound on Starr, while his friends drove away in his car.

Though most of the West had been tamed by the turn of the century, Arizona was still on the wild side in its remoter areas. These were cleaned up by the determined Arizona Rangers, who operated from 1901 to 1909 under the command of Captain Burton Mossman. Yet by then the telephone and telegraph had made it far more difficult for outlaws to vanish into the wilds, and lawmen, thanks to photographic files, knew what most badmen looked like. Jesse James had been able to dine in a hotel at the same table as a number of Pinkerton men – before the firm had developed its system of mug shots to perfection – without being detected.

Another symbolic moment came in 1911, when Oklahoma's last land rush took place, but as this book began with the first Americans, it should perhaps end with them, not so much out of sentiment, but because one of the stories in question, about two young Northern Cheyenne, tells more than many books about Indians in general and the Plains Indians in particular.

Incident at Lame Deer

It occurred in September 1890 just before Wounded Knee, though there was no link between the two events. The Indians involved were a 25-year-old troublemaker named Head Chief and John Young Mule, who was aged 13 or 14. The place was Lame Deer, Montana.

Head Chief's problem was that he had never been able to establish a reputation as a warrior. Times had changed. Chief American Horse had a daughter whom Head Chief was fond of and who told him that food was short in her father's lodge. So Head Chief went hunting with his young friend, an orphan.

Although they were after deer, they

246

shot a cow instead, whose owner was a settler called Gaffney. The settler's nephew, Hugh Boyle, suddenly rode up when the pair had finished butchering the cow. Boyle said something that Head Chief did not understand, but Young Mule did. He had been to school. 'He called us dogs,' he told his friend. So Head Chief shot Royle and buried him. Later, Young Mule would report that Boyle's exact words were: 'I see a hungry dog has snapped up one of our cows.'

It was not long before soldiers traced the culprit through his horse and bloodstains. As for the Cheyenne, they were expecting to be attacked.

On hearing this, Head Chief went to American Horse and told him what had happened. He asked him to tell the white soldiers that he was the killer. He refused to be hanged for his crime; instead he would fight them all.

Young Mule told his friend that he would die with him. The orphan boy said that when Head Chief was dead, he would have nothing. So the pair went up a hill and stayed there until dawn when it was time for them to die. They had their horses with them.

The sun came up on hundreds of Cheyenne below the hill and on white cavalry and infantry, prepared for an uprising. Down the hill charged the two young braves, then wheeled up again. On the way up, Young Mule's horse was hit and the boy had to lead it to the top, left it there, and charged down on foot, firing, darting left and right, taking cover, shooting once more and running towards the soldiers until he was killed.

Now Head Chief donned his grandfather's war bonnet and mounted his horse. He charged down towards the soldiers at a gallop. Bullets hit him

Opposite page: Henry Starr began his criminal career on horseback and ended it in automobiles. In 1921 he was mortally wounded in Arkansas.

Below: The 1893 land rush into Oklahoma, one of several which gave Indian lands to whites. Instant towns sprang up, Guthrie springing from nothing to 10,000 in a single day.

time and again, and he was still charging through the dismounted troopers when he was shot dead by an officer. An epic had ended.

Then the soldiers formed up and marched away. The Cheyenne were left with their dead.

Wounded Knee

There was nothing epic about the last battle of the Indian Wars. It was stark tragedy. As has been related, Sitting Bull crossed into Canada in 1877, where the North-West Mounted Police soon found themselves with 4,000 Sioux to deal with. Firmly but fairly, they did so, and a good relationship was formed between the no-nonsense Major Walsh and the great Hunkpapa Sioux leader.

In his famous book, *Bury My Heart at Wounded Knee*, Dee Brown fails to give the reasons why it became the Mounties' job to get the Sioux back across the international border. Simply, there was already such a shortage of buffalo that food for the Canadian Blackfoot and Cree was becoming a problem – which might result in raids south across the border. In addition the Blackfoot were not on good terms with the Sioux, with the resulting danger of warfare between the tribes.

It was harsh common sense to get the Sioux out of Canada, and in 1881 Sitting Bull followed others who had gone south, leading 186 followers to Fort Burford, Montana.

The then huge Sioux reservation was an unhappy place. Indians were meant to become as whites, ideally Christian farmers, and if they had other ideas, they were called 'non-progressives'. After two years as a prisoner, Sitting Bull was sent to Standing Rock, where the agent, James McLaughlin decided to lessen the great man's influence by appointing lesser men in his place.

Meanwhile, a new doctrine,

preached by genuine friends of the Indian as well as their greedy enemies, was the holding of land by individual Indians. In the tribe as a whole lay the Indians' power, a fact not understood by many champions of the Indian. As for their enemies, they could rejoice when the well-meaning Dawes Act of 1887 advised individual allotments for each Indian family but opened millions of acres of Indian land to the whites. In Dakota Territory this meant that the great Sioux Reservation would be turned into six small ones. An enormous 9 million acres (3,645,000 hectares) was handed over to white buyers.

At this grim moment the last of a long line of Indian messiahs appeared in Nevada, a Paiute Indian, Wovoka, who preached peace. A new world in which Indians would live without whites was dawning. They would meet their dead once more. And there was a dance for them to learn, a simple, holy 'Ghost' dance.

The Sioux, alas, began to believe that Wovoka preached war and that white bullets could not harm them if they wore 'Ghost Shirts'. Disease and short rations made them more desperate. Though there were now forts surrounding the reservation, war seemed a real possibility to the military.

Pine Ridge was the most explosive area, a good agent, Dr. Gillicuddy, having been replaced by Daniel Royer, a weak man who knew little of Indians. Panicking, he wired for troops.

Six hundred men were hastily sent to the Rosebud and Pine Ridge agencies, which caused some Sioux to come to them for safety and others to get as far away as possible and resume what was now undoubtedly a warlike dance. Newspapers meanwhile encouraged stories of a coming Indian war.

It was General Nelson Miles, commanding the Division of the Missouri, with his headquarters in Chicago, who ordered the arrest of Sitting Bull and the Minneconjou Chief Big Foot. Agent McLaughlin, having got the order he wanted, sent Indian police and troops to Sitting Bull's tent. The arrest was left to the Indians, who broke into the tent at dawn on December 15th, 1890. The great chief was seized, but his followers attempted to rescue him. During the fight that ensued, Sergeant Red Tomahawk

Above: An artist's impression of the tragic fight at Wounded Knee in 1890.

Left: The aftermath of Wounded Knee.

Right: Sergeant Red Tomahawk, the Indian policeman who shot Sitting Bull.

shot Sitting Bull dead. The police had to be saved by the white soldiers.

News of Sitting Bull's death caused some Indians to return to their reservations, fearful of being attacked. But Chief Big Foot was in the Dakota Badlands with some 350 Sioux, having fled when troops had come near his people. Now he was coming back, heading for Pine Ridge, when four troops of the Seventh Cavalry intercepted him on December 28th. The next day, Colonel James A. Forsyth surrounded the band with 500 backed up by four Hotchkiss rapid-firing guns. It was bitterly cold, with snow in the air, and nearby Wounded Knee Creek was covered by ice. Big Foot was in his tent, ill with pneumonia.

Forsyth ordered the Sioux to be disarmed and tension mounted, made worse by rumours that they would be sent to Florida in chains. Many of the troops were raw recruits. Few rifles were given up and the soldiers were ordered to close in, the warriors being out in a hollow square. Other soldiers were ordered to search the women for weapons.

The tension grew by the second when suddenly Yellow Bird, a medicine man, started dancing the Ghost Dance and calling that white bullets could not penetrate the men's Ghost Shirts. There was a scuffle as a soldier searched an Indian. A shot rang out and Yellow Bird threw some dust in the air. Some Sioux cast aside their blankets and raised their rifles as the soldiers opened fire. In a nightmare of dust, smoke, conbustion and noise, the last fight of the Indian Wars began.

Yet it was more a massacre than a battle, for half of Big Foot's warriors were killed at once in a blast of rifle fire. Those who survived fought like tigers, using knives and clubs if they had no rifles. Some women and children raced to join the fighting.

A desperate retreat followed to a ravine, the Hotchkiss guns pouring out shells as the Sioux made their last stand, singing their death songs. Soon it was all over. A blizzard set in and a blanket of snow covered the stricken ground. Twenty-five soldiers had been killed, more than 150 Indian men, women and children lay dead, while many of the survivors had terrible wounds. Wounded Knee was not planned genocide, but a tragic accident, yet the result was the same. The date was December 29th, 1890. The Ghost Shirts had failed and the long centuries of Indian Wars had finally come to an end in the Dakota snow.

Below: Chief Big Foot lying dead in the snow after the massacre at Wounded Knee.

INDEX

Figures in *italics* refer to illustrations.

BIBLIOGRAPHY

Berton, Pierre. *The Klondike Fever*, Knopf 1958: As *Klondike*, W.H. Allen 1960.

Billington, Ray Allen. *Westward Expansion*, Macmillan, New York 1949.

Bourke, John Gregory. *On the Border with Crook* (reprint), Rio Grande Press 1962.

Brandon, William. *The American Heritage Book of Indians*, American Heritage Publishing Co. 1961.

Davis, Britton. *The Truth about Geronimo*, Yale 1929; softback, 1963.

De Voto, Bernard. *Westward the Course of Empire*, Houghton Mills 1952; Eyre and Spottiswoode 1954.

De Voto: Editor. *The Journals of Lewis and Clark*, Houghton Mifflin 1953.

Dick, Everett. *The Sod-House Frontier, 1854–1890*, University of Nebraska Press 1979.

Foreman, Grant. *Indian Removal*, University of Oklahoma Press 1932/1976.

Forrest, Earle R. *Arizona's Dark and Bloody Ground*, Caxton Printers 1936.

Fulton, Maurice. *History of the Lincoln County War*, University of Arizona Press 1968.

Gard, Wayne. *Frontier Justice*, University of Oklahoma Press 1949.

Graymont, Barbara. *The Iroquois in the American Revolution*, Syracuse University Press 1972.

Greever, William S. *The Bonanza West*, University of Oklahoma Press 1963.

Hagan, William T. *American Indians* (revised edition), University of Chicago 1979.

Horgan, Paul. *Conquistadors in North America*, Macmillan 1963.

Jackson, Donald Dale. *Gold Dust*, Knopf 1980; George Allen and Unwin 1980.

James, Marquis. *The Raven: A Biography of Sam Houston*, Bobbs-Merrill 1929.

Keleher, William A. *The Violence in Lincoln County*, University of New Mexico Press 1957.

Klinck, Carl F. Editor. *Tecumseh, Fact and Fiction in early records*, Prentice Hall 1961.

Lavender, David. *Westward Vision*, McGraw Hill 1963; Eyre and Spottiswoode 1965.

Peckham, Howard. *Pontiac and the Indian Uprising*, Princeton University Press 1947.

Rosa, Joseph G. *They Called Him Wild Bill*, University of Oklahoma Press 1964 and 1974.

Shirley, Glenn. *The Law West of Fort Smith*, University of Oklahoma Press 1968.

Sonnichsen, C.L. *Roy Bean, Law West of the Pecos*. The Devin-Adair Co. 1943.

Stewart, Edgar I. *Custer's Luck*, University of Oklahoma Press 1955.

Trapp, Dan L. *The Conquest of Apacheria*, University of Oklahoma Press 1967.

Turner III, Frederick William. *The Portable North American Indian Reader*, Viking Press 1974.

Utley, Robert. *Frontiersmen in Blue, The United States Army and the Indian, 1848–1865*, Macmillan 1967.

Utley, Robert M. *Frontier Regulars, The United States Army and the Indian, 1866–1890*, Macmillan 1973.

Utley, Robert M. *The Last Days of the Sioux Nation*, Yale University Press 1963.

Van Every, Dale. *A Company of Heroes*, William Morrow 1962.

Webb, Walter Prescott. *The Texas Rangers*, University of Texas Press 1966.

The Old West series published by Time-Life cannot be too strongly recommended visually, though, inevitably, some texts are better than others.

The most complete series ever published on Indians is The University of Oklahoma's 'Civilization of the American Indian', now heading for the 200 mark. Grant Foreman's book, *Indian Removal*, noted above, was Number 2.